sharing Through song

my eternal family

sharing through song

my eternal family

written by
Alison Palmer

illustrated by
Debra stinson

HORIZON PUBLISHERS
Springville, Utah

ISBN: 978-0-88290-953-0

Published by Horizon Publishers, an imprint of Cedar Fort, Inc., 2373 W. 700 S., Springville, UT, 84663
Distributed by Cedar Fort, Inc., www.cedarfort.com

Cover design by Nicole Williams
Cover design © 2008 by Lyle Mortimer
Edited and typeset by Allison M. Kartchner

Printed in the United States of America

10   9   8   7   6   5   4   3   2   1

Printed on acid-free paper

contents

ACKnowledgments

Many thanks to Duane and Jean Crowther of Horizon Publishers, for continuing to have faith in my work. Great appreciation is also extended to my Cedar Fort family, especially Heather Holm and Allison Kartchner for patiently keeping me in line and putting up with all my "oops, didn't I fix that?" moments.

Thankfulness and love are also expressed to my husband, who always cares more about my word count for the day than whether I remembered to do the dishes, or shower for that matter! He keeps putting up with me book after book and still manages to love me. It's nothing short of a miracle some days.

Thanks, as well, to Debra Stinson for her continued dedication and hard work creating the beautiful illustrations that add so much to my words. No matter how full life gets, she always comes through for me.

Most of all, I must express my love and gratitude toward my Heavenly Father. He continues to bless me, even when it has been undeserved. He filled my soul with the thoughts and ideas that became this book. He sends the Spirit to quietly burn within my heart, continually reminding me how much I love this gospel. Then He nudges me to share that feeling the best ways I can. Through His inspiration, may the lives of many children be blessed.

how to use this book

Most of us have traditionally separated sharing time into a short lesson and a music time. We have been asked by the General Primary Board to use the full thirty minutes for sharing time; music is integrated throughout. (See "Instructions for Sharing Time," *2009 Outline for Sharing Time and the Children's Sacrament Meeting Presentation,* 1.) This is not always easy. Compliance requires early preparation and more communication and cooperation between presidencies and choristers, but it works!

Music teaches where words fail, and if we do not merge the two, we are missing beautiful opportunities to teach our children things they will always remember. The overall goal of sharing time should be to teach the gospel and build testimonies. *Sharing Through Song* works on this philosophy. Children must first hear the gospel and then sing the gospel. When these two work together, our children will feel the Spirit and know the gospel is true.

This manual is designed to help those who desire to follow the guidance of our leaders to the best of their ability. However, it has limitless potential. These lessons are built around inviting the Spirit through the use of scriptures and song. Please feel free to mold these lessons to fit your needs as a leader, teacher, or parent.

The lessons in this volume are intended to help focus your efforts in teaching songs and gospel concepts related to eternal families. There are two lessons for each topic. One lesson teaches the message of one specific song. The second lesson reinforces the topic through multiple songs. For your convenience, complete instructions, a list of materials, and illustrations are included with each lesson.

Please also keep in mind that this is copyrighted material intended for use within the purchaser's home or Primary only. If you enjoy using it, share the information with your friends, but allow them to show honesty by purchasing their own copy of this manual.

May the Lord bless you in your endeavors to serve His children.

1. I Lived in heaven

Children's Songbook, 4

Opening Song: "I Am a Child of God," *Children's Songbook,* 2
Closing Song: "I Lived in Heaven," *Children's Songbook,* 4

materials needed

- Copies, one for each child, of the word prompt page from this lesson
- Scissors
- Stapler
- Crayons or color pencils for the children to use
- *Old Testament Stories* (Salt Lake City: The Church of Jesus Christ of Latter-day Saints, 1980), preferably video/dvd, but book may be used (available from Church Distribution Centers)

preparation

- Preview and prepare your video or book to show the story of the premortal life.
- Cut apart the word prompt page along the lines.
- Staple the pages together in the order of the song words.

Teaching suggestions

Begin by showing the story of the premortal life and the presentation of Heavenly Father's plan for us, stopping after Jesus Christ is appointed to be our Savior.

The children will learn a song today that talks about the story they just heard concerning their time with Heavenly Father before they came to this earth. In order for them to make a more personal connection with the message, the children will illustrate their own word-prompt booklets for the song. Help the children make the association between the story they just heard and how it is described in the song. Repeat the words to each verse with the children several times, and try singing the verse once before moving on to the next verse.

After all three verses have been reviewed in this manner, testify that each one of us truly was present in heaven before we came to earth; we were part of the things they have been singing about. Emphasize that we are all children of God and that the plan you have been talking about was set up for our happiness here on earth and to make it possible for us to return to Heavenly Father after we leave this earth.

Pass out the word-prompt booklets to the children. Tell the children that they will create their own storybook for the song, drawing pictures of themselves in heaven. Go through each page of words again, talking about what they mean and inviting the children to spend a few minutes drawing their own picture to represent the line on each sheet.

After the children have drawn their pictures, sing the entire song again, letting the children use their personal books as music prompts.

If time allows, invite children to come to the front and hold up pictures out of their books to prompt all of the children in singing the song a final time.

I lived in heaven a long time ago, it is true;

Then Heav'nly Father presented a beautiful plan

Father said he needed someone who had enough love

Lived there and loved there with people I know. So did you.

There was another who sought for the honor divine.

All about earth and eternal salvation for man.

Jesus was chosen, and as the Messiah he came,

To give his life so we all could return there above.

Giving us hope of a wonderful life yet to be

Jesus said, "Father, send me, and the glory be thine."

Conquering evil and death through his glorious name,

Home in that heaven where Father is waiting for me.

2. I Am a Child of God

Opening Song: "I Know My Father Lives," *Children's Songbook,* 5
Closing Song: "I Am a Child of God," *Children's Songbook,* 2

Materials Needed

- Gospel Art Kit (GAK) 240 (Jesus the Christ)
- 6 manila file folders
- Glue
- Scissors
- Copies of the large illustrations on cardstock (2 copies of the illustration of Jesus Christ)
- 3 copies of the double pop-up templates on cardstock
- Copies of the single pop-up template for each child
- Small pictures of Christ, if you have access to an LDS bookstore or Church Distribution Center, or copies of the small Jesus Christ illustration; enough for each child to have one small picture
- Thumbtacks or other fasteners
- Chalkboard
- Chalk
- Crayons or colored pencils for the children to use
- Glue sticks for the children to use
- Picture of yourself as either a child or adult

Preparation

- Cut apart the illustrations.
- Cut the three cardstock pop-up templates down the middle dotted line.
- Cut all the templates along the inside dotted lines.
- Fold the cut portion of the cardstock templates out at the ends of the lines on top and bottom.
- Fold the pop-ups in half, horizontally, on the solid line, keeping the tab portion separated on its original folds.
- Crease the cut tab flat after the template has been folded; this creates a pop-up stand.
- Glue a pop-up stand inside of each folder, match the main folds, and leave the cut-out stand free from glue.
- Glue the "baby" version of each plant or animal on the outside of a file folder.
- Glue the matching "adult" to the cut-out stand inside the folder, arranging it so that the base of the picture is slightly above the bottom cut-out fold.
- The children will make pop-up booklets by folding a full-page template in half length-wise on the line and then again horizontally so that the cut tab folds out on the inside as the larger templates did.

Teaching Suggestions

Show the pop-ups one at a time and ask the children what the item on the front will become. When the correct answer is guessed, open the pop-up for the children to see, and then tack it up on the board. Talk about some of the things that each baby would need to learn as it grows up.

Sing the corresponding song before moving on to the next folder. Show all of the plants and animals first.

Next, show the picture of baby Jesus in the manger. Help the children recognize that this is a special baby, and ask them to tell you who He will grow up to be. Put away the illustrated pop-up, and have the children refocus on GAK 240 as you talk about some of the things that make Jesus Christ special.

Help the children understand that Jesus Christ is Heavenly Father's firstborn son and His literal son here on this earth. Sing: "He Sent His Son," *Children's Songbook*, 34.

Finally, show the picture of yourself and ask the children who they think you should grow up to be like. After they have given their answers, show the inside pop-up and share your desire to be like Jesus Christ.

Refocus their attention to the GAK, to keep a more realistic idea of Jesus Christ in the children's minds. Emphasize that each of us is also a unique child of God, just as Jesus was. Heavenly Father gave us this earth so that we could come here to gain bodies, learn, and grow to be more like Him.

Heavenly Father sent Jesus to earth to help us understand how we could learn and grow. Jesus Christ also atoned for our sins so that we can overcome our sins and be the kind of people Heavenly Father wants us to be.

Use the chalkboard to list some things the children can tell you about Jesus Christ, which can help them understand what Heavenly Father is like. Emphasize that we should all strive to be like Jesus Christ as much as we can.

Help the children understand that just as every creature you talked about started out different, and grew up into something different, each child of God is different as well. Heavenly Father has blessed each of us with different talents and abilities that we can develop as we try to be more like Him. We can learn to be more loving and more forgiving, we may be blessed with abilities that let us help others, or we may be blessed so that it is easy for us to learn new things. No matter where we start from, if we try to be more like Jesus every day, we are growing up to be like our Heavenly Father. That is the goal of this life.

Sing: "I'm Trying to Be like Jesus," *Children's Songbook*, 78.

Help the children recognize the presence of the Spirit and share a brief testimony of these gospel truths.

Pass out the pop-up cards and crayons. Show the children how to fold the paper to make a card. Instruct the children to draw their own picture on the outside and write on the bottom of the inside a quality of Jesus Christ that they would like to have as they try to grow to be like Him.

Next, give them a copy of the picture of Jesus and help them understand how to glue it to the inside to make their own pop-up to take home.

Pop-ups and Suggested Corresponding Songs

- Seed and Tree: "Faith," *Children's Songbook*, 96
- Egg and Bird: "In the Leafy Treetops," *Children's Songbook*, 240
- Duckling and Duck: "Happy Song," *Children's Songbook*, 264
- Caterpillar and Butterfly: "My Heavenly Father's World," *Children's Songbook*, 228 (verse 2)
- Manger and Jesus: "He Sent His Son," *Children's Songbook*, 34
- Yourself and Jesus: "I'm Trying to Be like Jesus," *Children's Songbook*, 78

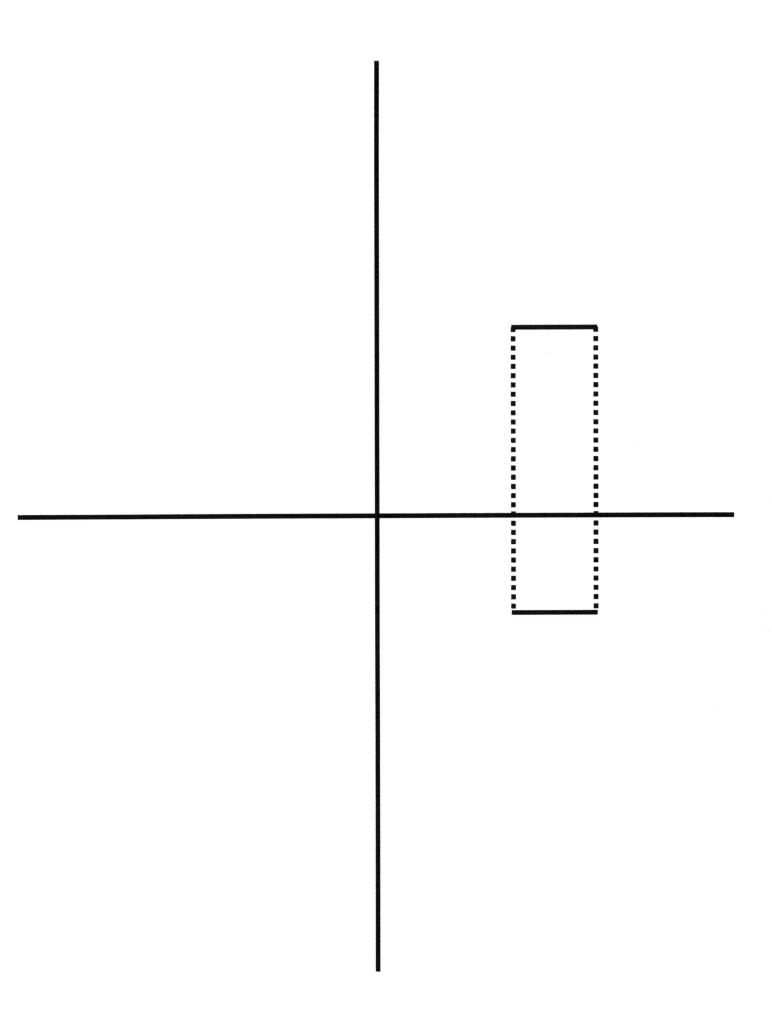

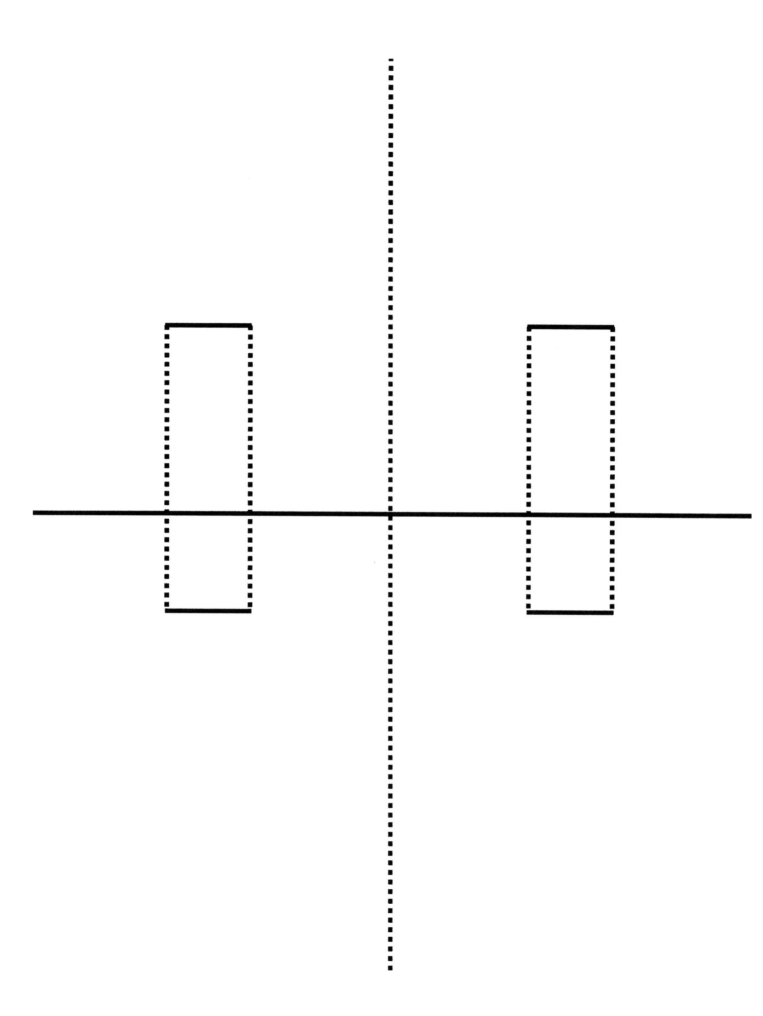

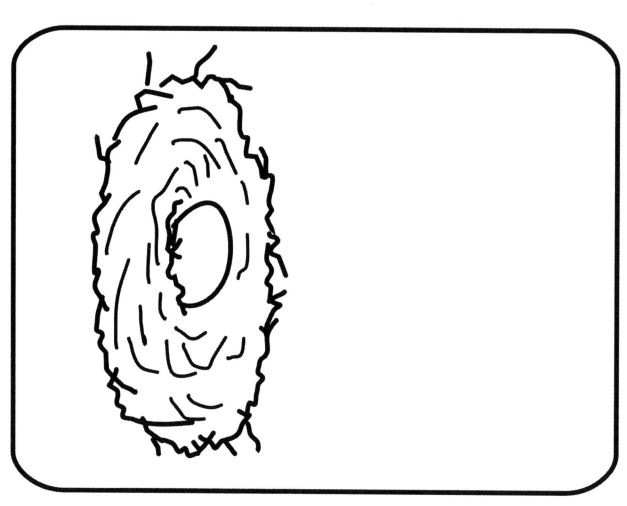

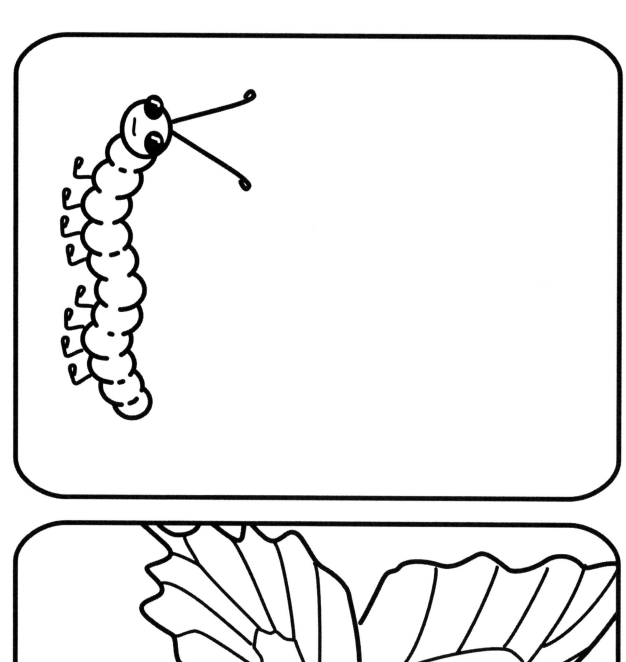
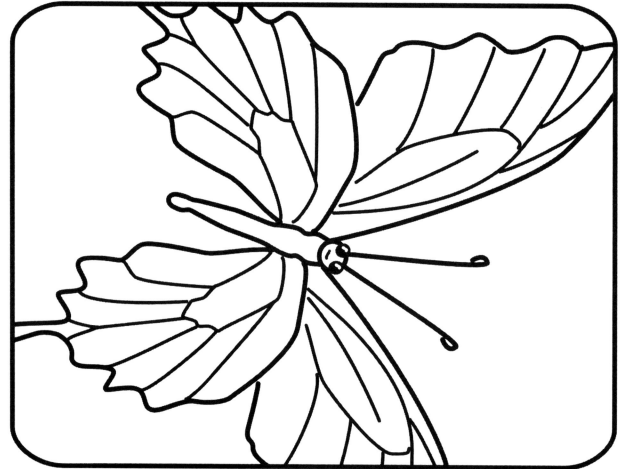

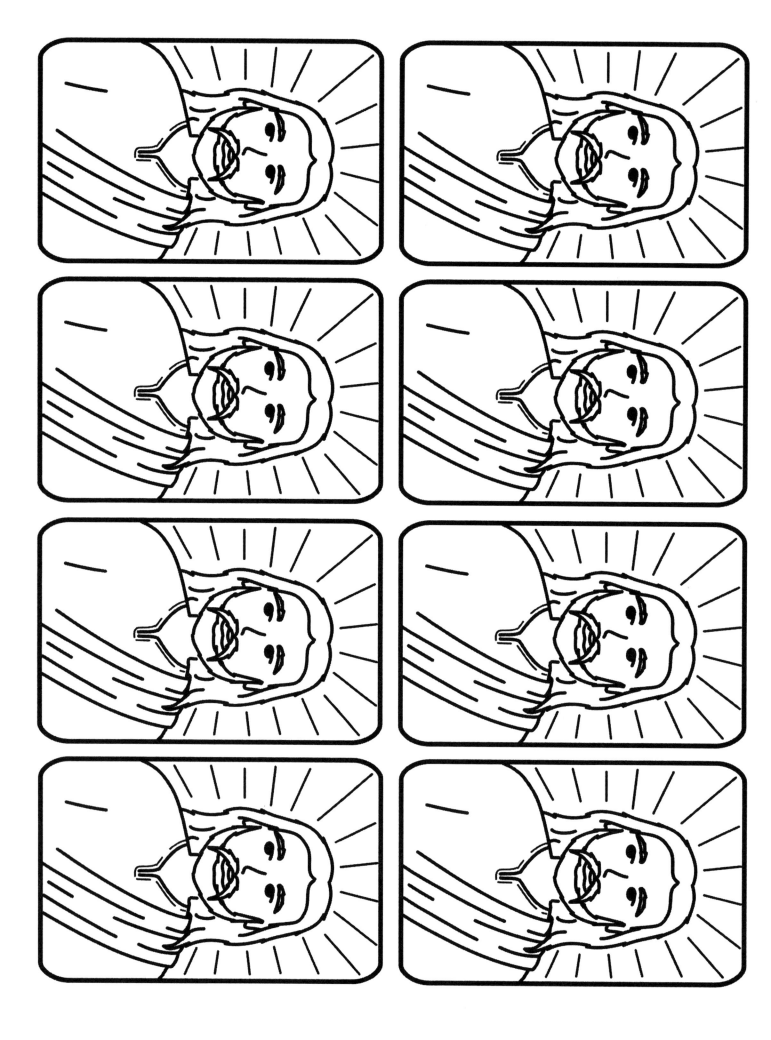

3. how firm a foundation

Hymns, no. 85

Opening Song: "The Wise Man and the Foolish Man," *Children's Songbook,* 281
Closing Song: "How Firm a Foundation," *Hymns*, no. 85, verses 1 and 3

materials needed

- Gospel Art Kit (GAK) 403 (The First Vision)
- Picture of Thomas S. Monson
- Copies of Thomas S. Monson, "Come Listen to a Prophet's Voice: A Treasure Map," *Friend*, Sept. 2004, 2; and Thomas S. Monson, "Come Listen to a Prophet's Voice: The Race," *Friend*, June 2004, 2
- Copy of the song phrase assignments for reference
- At least 8 children's wooden building blocks
- 3 or 4 large marshmallows
- Small display table

preparation

- Read and be familiar with the two articles from President Monson.
- Build a small pyramid of blocks on the display table.

teaching suggestions

Introduce the new song by asking the children to relay the gospel message that they think the opening song teaches. Show them your block pyramid. Ask the children if they think it looks like it has a firm foundation. (Yes.) Next ask the children what they think would happen if you tried to replace the lowest blocks with a row of marshmallows. What difference would it make in the way the pyramid stood, its stability, and its ability to be enlarged if you wanted to make the pyramid bigger? (The marshmallows are much softer and less stable; they are unable to hold their shape after a time.)

Next, show the picture of President Monson and explain that you are going to read them a short message from the prophet that talks about building firm foundations that will last. Read "Come Listen to a Prophet's Voice: A Treasure Map." Allow the children to briefly discuss the three principles that President Monson says we need in order to find good treasures and happiness. Then, bring the children back to his first point: "Learn from the past."

Show the GAK picture of the First Vision and ask the children why they think this particular moment in history is so important and what they can learn from it. Testify of the First Vision and the Restoration of the gospel, then ask the children if they can think of other gospel blessings and principles they can build on because of the Restoration. These should include the Book of Mormon, a living prophet, priesthood keys, temples, and anything else the children are grateful to have as members of Christ's true church.

Explain that they will learn a song today to help them remember President Monson's message to build on firm foundations and to seek heavenly treasures that will make us happy and lead us back to Heavenly Father.

Divide the children into boys and girls. Explain that Heavenly Father wants all members of a family to work together to be righteous and get back to Him. The boys and girls will represent two different parts of a family, such as a husband and wife, or a brother and sister. Each group will have special responsibilities in order to learn the song, and they must learn to work together in order to sing it completely.

Start with the boys: give them the words to their first assigned line. Repeat it with them, then let them hear what the melody sounds like. Next, have the boys try to repeat their words once again, and then sing along with the melody. Tell them they must remember their part while you teach the girls their part.

Follow the same procedure with the girls, teaching them the second line.

Next, explain how the two lines work together to create the first part of the new song. If they follow the song, the boys will have to sing their words first, and then wait quietly as the girls sing their words. Review each group's parts with them once again, then let them try putting the two parts together, each singing their own line. Commend the children for their efforts to work together and sing.

Explain that the next line of the song with be sung by both the girls and boys. It is a responsibility that must be shared in order to complete the singing task well. Share the words and melody to the combined line and practice it several times.

Now tell the children that they will have a small contest. They will sing the song again, from the beginning, with both of the parts and the combined section they have learned. You and the other leaders will be listening to see who is singing the best. That group will earn a block to build their own tower with on their side of the display table.

After each part is sung, make your judgments and assess for any review needs, then award a block from your pyramid to the appropriate side.

Repeat this same learning procedure for each new set of phrases, having the children "compete" against each other in singing participation. For these judgments, only the phrases currently being taught should be included in the singing.

After each set of phrases from both verse one and three have been reviewed in this manner, go back to the beginning and review the song in its entirety one time. Then, for the final competition, the children will sing the whole song with their assigned parts.

You will then choose a reverent child from the "winning" side to come forward. He must pick someone from the other team to come to the front and help quietly rebuild a larger pyramid using all the blocks you brought. While the children are building, the rest of the children will try singing the whole song, with every child singing all the parts.

Remind the children that even though one side may have gotten more blocks for their small individual towers, they could not have sung the entire song by themselves or build a very big tower until they worked with the other team. Every person in a family has different strengths and weaknesses: when we all work together and support each other, we build the most solid foundations.

End by showing the picture of President Monson again. Tell the children he has one more important message for the children about firm foundations. Read "Come Listen to a Prophet's Voice: The Race."

Remind the children to find love and support from their family members as they try to live the principles of the restored gospel. Every time they do this, they are replacing a marshmallow with a building block and making their way back to Heavenly Father with an eternal family.

4. Let's Glue the Family Together

Opening Song: "Love Is Spoken Here," *Children's Songbook*, 190
Closing Song: "Here We Are Together," *Children's Songbook*, 261

Materials Needed

- Small object for children to pass around, such as a beanbag
- Empty container (to hold strips of paper)
- Copy of song choices
- Glue stick
- Copy of the family picture printed on cardstock
- Copy of puzzle outline on cardstock
- Scissors

Preparation

- Cut apart the song choices and place them into your container.
- Assemble the illustrations.
- Color the family picture as needed and cut it into its separate puzzle pieces.

Teaching Suggestions

Because Heavenly Father loves His children so much, He wants us to return to live with Him. Eternal families are one of the most important parts of that plan. Everything else Heavenly Father asks of us should help strengthen those bonds as a family and our own personal testimonies. Share with the children that today you will be discussing some of the many things Heavenly Father has given us as examples and instructions on how to have a happy, eternal family.

Identify the first song you have chosen to sing and explain that you will be playing a version of Hot Potato. The children will pass your chosen object around the room while singing the identified song. The pianist will stop at a random interval in the song. When the pianist stops playing, the child holding the object must say what the next word(s) in the song would be. If they get the word(s) right, they get to glue a piece of the family picture on to the poster board (matching the outlines to the chosen puzzle piece for placement). Then have the children finish singing the entire song.

Discuss what each song teaches us about the importance of families, either through the scripture story it talks about or the general message of the song. A child who can tell you what lessons for the family that they can learn from this song gets to choose the next song from the container.

Continue in this manner until all the pieces have been glued in place. Help the children understand that being part of a happy family means learning to follow the example of Jesus Christ and other righteous families in the scriptures. As we try to help each other live righteously, we become closer and stronger as a family. Every time we do something to strengthen our family, we are adding a little glue that can hold us together as the eternal families Heavenly Father intends us to be. Bear testimony of the importance of families and encourage the children in their own efforts to "glue" their families together.

Suggested Songs about Families

- "I Am a Child of God," *Children's Songbook*, 2
- "Love Is Spoken Here," *Children's Songbook*, 190
- "A Happy Family," *Children's Songbook*, 198
- "I Love to See the Temple," *Children's Songbook*, 95
- "Follow the Prophet," *Children's Songbook*, 110, verses 1, 3, 6, and 9
- "Quickly, I'll Obey," *Children's Songbook*, 197
- "I Have a Family Tree," *Children's Songbook*, 199
- "We'll Bring the World His Truth (Army of Helaman)," *Children's Songbook*, 172
- "Book of Mormon Stories," *Children's Songbook*, 118, verses 3 and 8
- "I'm Trying to Be like Jesus," *Children's Songbook*, 78

5. fathers

Children's Songbook, 209

Opening Song: "My Dad," *Children's Songbook,* 211
Closing Song: "Fathers," *Children's Songbook,* 209

materials needed

- Dress-up clothes for the children to use (suit coat, man's shoes, tie, pants with belt)
- Book of Mormon

preparation

- Review Mosiah 4:14–15.

teaching suggestions

Share the scripture from Mosiah with the children. Help them understand that these verses represent some of the things Heavenly Father has asked our parents to do for us. Ask them if they can name some of the things they heard.

Continue the discussion by specifically talking about the many ways that fathers can bless our homes. Explain to the children that "father" can mean several things in the song that they will learn, but the things fathers do are the same. A father is someone who loves his children and tries his best to help them be good, happy people.

Express your gratitude for the quiet example of fathers. Tell the children that today they will try to fill a father's shoes by being an example and guide in Primary. They will take turns dressing up like a "father" and help you lead the singing.

Explain that sometimes we can show others good things without saying a word. A conductor, who leads an orchestra or choir, does this. Ask the children if they have ever heard a conductor shouting over the music to tell the players how the music should go during a performance. Ask them to demonstrate what he does do. Do they know why he does this? He is showing with his hands how the music should be played.

Tell the children that they will learn one way to conduct this song. It's as simple as counting to two. Ask the children to clap their hands and repeat steadily "one—two."

Show the children that this song follows a very steady rhythm that only changes slightly. To do this, have the piano play the song one time through. Invite the children to see if they can find and clap the steady beat that the music keeps.

Introduce the first phrase of the song. Have the children try singing this line along with you, then try clapping along as well. Help them begin to feel the beat of the music and its correlation with the words they are singing. Draw a wide "U" on the chalkboard and trace over it from side to side as they clap and sing each word.

Tell the children that although this is a simpler pattern, this is the same method than a real conductor uses to keep the beat of the song so that the musicians and singers know how fast they should go.

Have reverent children come to the front to play the role of "father." They will put on the provided dress-up clothes and help you conduct each phrase of the song as it is learned.

Continue introducing new phrases by having the children clap and repeat the words, and then try having the children direct and sing the words. Start at the beginning and review the things you have learned at the end of every verse.

Children can also answer questions about the song, or fill in phrases for you, to earn opportunities to be the conducting father.

End with your testimony of the importance of a father's example to help us know how to choose the right.

6. Special Kinds of Families

Opening Song: "Love One Another," *Children's Songbook,* 136
Closing Song: "God Is Watching Over All," *Children's Songbook,* 229

Materials Needed

- Obtain copies of the *Friend* magazine articles listed in the lesson either from the actual magazine or from the archives on www.lds.org
- Paper and crayons as needed for the class presentations

Preparation

- Prayerfully evaluate the appropriateness of each story suggested for your Primary children and choose the most effective ones for your situations. If there are other special situations that need to be addressed in your own unit, utilize the search feature on www.lds.org to find a suitable story from the *Friend* that will help you speak to this need.

Teaching Suggestions

Begin by explaining that while Heavenly Father has set the pattern for what a "forever family" is to be like, there are many forms that a family can take here on earth. Be sensitive to the fact that although Heavenly Father would like to have every child in a home with two parents, this is not always possible as we experience the trials and challenges we were sent to earth to experience. Heavenly Father is aware of each of His children, and He tries to bless them with the best family situations He can. Help the children understand that they will be "meeting" several different children from the *Friend* magazine who can help them understand these special kinds of families and the blessings they can bring into a child's life.

Separate the children into their classes or other appropriate groupings, giving each group one article to review. Have their teacher or leader read the assigned story. Next, have the children discuss what the family in the story is like, who it consists of, and how they love and help each other. If actual copies of the *Friend* magazines are not available to use, for more genuine illustrations, have the children each draw a picture of what they think the child or family in the story could look like. They will hold their pictures for the other children while briefly sharing what they have learned about families from their story. After each account is finished, emphasize any points you feel that are important for your Primary children to understand about the story, sing the assigned song, and move to the next group.

End with your testimony of families and an assurance that Heavenly Father loves and cares for each of His children. He tries very hard to surround them with people who will love and care for them. This doesn't always mean the same thing for every family. The important thing is to love your family and help them be the best they can be. Emphasize that after we leave this life, if we have lived worthy of "forever family" blessings, Heavenly Father will provide the best solutions and family units in the celestial kingdom as well. Also encourage the children to be kind, understanding, and respectful to those they know whose families are special and different.

Special Articles from the Friend Magazine

- Adopted Children: Jana Jones Steed, "Adopted," *Friend*, Aug. 1991, 43. Sing: "I Am a Child of God," *Children's Songbook*, 2.
- Divorce and the Ward Family: Kristen Chandler, "Ties that Bind," *Friend*, Jan. 2008, 20–22. Sing: "Fathers," *Children's Songbook*, 209.
- Foster Children: Kay Timpson, "Lacy's Talent," *Friend*, Jan. 2002, 43. Sing: "Every Star is Different," *Children's Songbook*, 142.
- Inviting Others to Be Part of Your Family: Frances Reimers-Smith, "Library Grandma," *Friend*, Mar. 1994, 46. Sing: "I'll Walk with You," *Children's Songbook*, 140.
- Living with Extended Family: Melvin Leavitt, "Adjoa Darkoa Asare-Addo of Accra, Ghana," *Friend*, Oct. 2000, 27. Sing: "I Have a Family Tree," *Children's Songbook*, 199.
- Living with Grandparents: M. L. Lowry, "'Where There's a Will,'" *Friend*, Sept. 1989, 8. Sing: "A Happy Family," *Children's Songbook*, 198 (using the alternate words grandma and grandpa)
- Older Relatives Staying in the Home: Alison M. Palmer, "Helping Grandma," *Friend*, Oct. 2005, 18. Sing: "A Special Gift Is Kindness," *Children's Songbook*, 145.
- Stepparents: Kimberly Webb, "A Forever Family—Julischka Schlatter of Möhlin, Switzerland," *Friend*, May 2006, 18–20. Sing: "I Love to See the Temple," *Children's Songbook*, 95.

7. Beautiful Savior

Children's Songbook, 62

Opening Song: "My Heavenly Father Loves Me," *Children's Songbook,* 228
Closing Song: "Beautiful Savior," *Children's Songbook,* 62

materials needed

- A large selection of Gospel Art Kit (GAK) pictures of Christ, including 201 (The Nativity), 221 (The Ten Lepers), 223 (Triumphal Entry), 233 (Mary and the Resurrected Lord), 240 (Jesus the Christ), 317 (Jesus Healing the Nephites), and 403 (The First Vision)
- Colored chalk and chalkboard
- Small, sturdy step stool for the children to use

preparation

- If your unit's chalkboard is not compatible with colored chalk, try to obtain a sheet of butcher paper and crayons for the children to use. Mount the paper over the chalkboard or other large display area.
- Place the following in this order: GAK 204, 317, 403, 201, 221, 223, 233, and keep them separated to use with the last verse.
- Place the remaining pictures of Jesus Christ along the bottom of the chalkboard in the chalk tray.

teaching suggestions

Help the children recall some of the things they sang about in the opening song, discussing how or why these things might help us remember how much Heavenly Father loves us. Heavenly Father wanted the earth to be beautiful and full of blessings for His children. He wanted them to have everything they would need to live and be happy while they were away from Him. Help the children understand that Jesus Christ followed Heavenly Father's instructions to create this beautiful world for all of us. We can see Their love for us in many things around us everyday. Continue the same line of thought by having the children name some of their favorite things, just as the opening song did, that help them remember Heavenly Father and Jesus Christ.

Explain that the children will learn a song today that talks about some beautiful things to enjoy on earth, and help the children understand the happy, peaceful feelings that these beautiful things can spark in each one of us. Those feelings of happiness, peace, and love tell us that Heavenly Father and Jesus Christ are real, that They love us, and that They know us by name. That it is important for us to try and live the way They would want us to, so we can live with Them again. These feelings help us form our testimonies of the gospel and it's most central figure: Jesus Christ. Introduce the name of the song as you show them GAK 240.

Introduce the first phrase of the song, "Fair is the sunshine." Explain that "fair," as used in the song, can mean something good and beautiful. Ask the children to briefly share some of the things that make the sunshine good and beautiful. Then, invite one child to come forward and stand on your stool to draw a sun on the upper left-hand side of your chalkboard.

Introduce the next phrase, "Fairer the moonlight." Repeat the process of discussing the moon's importance. Then have a child draw a moon next to the sun. Add the stars and discuss the next portion of the song. Then have the children learn to sing that portion of the song using the picture prompts they drew.

Introduce the next portion of the song, which talks about the Savior, as a whole unit. Discuss why it is true that Jesus would be more important and beautiful than the things they previously sang about.

Divide the last section into its three parts and ask three children to come up and choose their favorite picture of Christ to hold up. These pictures will help prompt the children for the last part of the song. As they choose, ask the children why they like or chose that particular picture.

Have the children stand just to the side of the drawn pictures. Hold up each picture and repeat the phrase that will go with that picture for the children to practice. Write a cue above each child's head (such as brighter, purer, love), in line with the previous illustrations, to also act as a prompt. Repeat the phrases about Jesus as a whole again, try singing this portion, and then practice putting the whole verse together.

Repeat this same process for the second verse of "Beautiful Savior," drawing simple illustrations for the items found in nature and choosing pictures of Christ to represent the most important message. Place these illustrations and word prompts slightly below the information for the first verse.

Be mindful of the Spirit in the room and help the children identify the feelings from the Holy Ghost that help them know how much they love Jesus Christ. Help them understand that as they have these feelings when they are learning about Jesus or His gospel, or when they are trying to live as He did, they are building their own testimony of Jesus Christ.

End by showing the children your separate stack of pictures that will be used as prompts for the final verses. Explain that you chose them because they are beautiful to you, but they also will help the children understand the final messages of the song.

Show each picture as you share its corresponding phrase, briefly explaining the connection as suggested in this lesson. Then, have the children review and try to sing the final verse while you hold up each picture to guide them through the message.

As a final step, call up six more children to hold pictures of Christ (away from the written word prompts) while the children try to sing the song in its entirety.

End by encouraging the children to remember the thoughts and feelings they have had while learning this song. As they learn and grow more, if they will always search out the things that bring them closer to the Savior, they will build strong testimonies that can help them find happiness.

suggested phrasing, verse three

- "Beautiful Savior!" GAK 240.
- "Lord of the nations!" GAK 317. Jesus Christ loves and cares for everyone, no matter where they live in the world.
- "Son of God" GAK 403. Jesus is Heavenly Father's firstborn son. Jesus carried His father's divinity with Him when He came to live on earth. God is Jesus' father in heaven and on earth.
- "And Son of Man!" GAK 201. Jesus also had an earthly mother and father so he could gain a body, learn, and grow just like every person who comes to earth.
- "Thee will I honor," GAK 221. When we honor someone, we recognize what they have done for us and our love for them.
- "Praise, and" GAK 223. We want Jesus and everyone around us to know how happy we are to have Him as our Savior and Friend.
- "Give glory," GAK 233. We also need to recognize His divinity and the great gifts He has given us.
- "Give praise and glory evermore! Evermore!" GAK 240.

("Beautiful Savior," *Children's Songbook*, 62)

8. White as Snow

Opening Song: "When I Am Baptized," *Children's Songbook,* 103
Closing Song: "Before I Take the Sacrament," *Children's Songbook,* 73

Materials Needed

- Gospel Art Kit (GAK) 604 (Passing the Sacrament)
- *Gospel Principles* book
- Copies of the included snowflake illustration, both sides
- Scissors
- Tape or pushpins
- String
- Chalk and chalkboard
- A picture of a snow scene
- Scriptures

Preparation

- Prayerfully review chapter 19, "Repentance," *Gospel Principles* (Salt Lake City: The Church of Jesus Christ of Latter-day Saints, 1997), 122, in order to find the best ways to explain the process to your Primary children.
- Color the front (blank) side of each snowflake red as needed.
- Cut out the snowflakes.
- Attach a long piece of string to the backside (with words) of the snowflake.
- Attach the other end of the string to the top of the chalkboard, forming a row of hanging snow-flakes.
- Flip all the snowflakes so that the red side is showing.

Teaching Suggestions

Ask the children to describe what they think is wrong with your snowflakes. Let them briefly discuss what snow is supposed to look like. Take a moment to describe a first snowfall. Show the children your picture of snow. Talk about the beauty of the snow as it covers the earth. Explain that after awhile, though, the snow will get tracked in, shoveled, salted, and in other ways dirtied. Soon, the snow that was very white and bright is not like that anymore.

Remind the children of the opening song. Ask them to tell you what the song was about. It talks about wanting to be clean and pure. It's a message of hope that your sins that make your spirit begin to gray and feel less clean can be washed away during the ordinance of baptism.

Help the children understand that when they came to earth as a baby, their spirit was just like newly fallen snow. We came here from living with Heavenly Father, so as babies we are very clean and pure. Our goodness radiates Heavenly Father's love for us. But as we get older, we make mistakes in our spiritual learning, just like we make mistakes as we are learning to walk or learning a new skill at school. Heavenly Father understands that these first mistakes are just part of learning. We don't know everything we need to know about following Heavenly Father when we are a very small child.

Eventually we reach an age where we are more responsible and know most things that we need to about what is right and wrong. This is called the age of accountability. It is also the time when we can be baptized. Ask the children to tell you what this age is.

Read Isaiah 1:18 with the children. Help them understand that the Atonement of Jesus Christ is what makes it possible for us to take something that has gotten dirty and make it clean again. It's not exactly like adding a new layer of snow over an old one. When we are baptized Jesus Christ makes our own snow, the spirit we were born with, clean and new again, just as it was when we were born.

Ask the children what they think happens next. Will their spirit stay clean forever? No. We continue to learn and grow, and we will still make mistakes. Our spirit "snow" will still change. It can still get muddy and dirty when we do something that is wrong.

Explain that each person can only be baptized once. Ask them how they think they would be able to turn their snow white again after they have already been baptized. Help them understand that Heavenly Father gave us the process of repentance to help us turn our snow over to Jesus Christ for Him to cleanse once again with the Atonement. Every time we realize that our snow has become red, or even just a little gray, we can repent and become pure and clean again.

Show GAK 604 and ask the children to explain to you what is happening in it. Help the children understand that the sacrament acts as our reminder to think about the promises we made to Heavenly Father when we were baptized. We promised to always remember Jesus Christ and try to be like Him. Taking the sacrament reminds us to see how we've been doing with those promises. We can think about all that the Savior has done for us, and check our spirit for any dirty spots that we might need to fix with repentance.

At this point summarize the different topics you have discussed: birth, baptism, repentance, and the sacrament. Help the children understand that all of these things are gifts that remind us of all that the Savior has done to help us get back to Heavenly Father again.

Explain that underneath your snowflakes are more things to help them understand how to use the Atonement to be white as snow. Each snowflake either has a part of the repentance process or a song to sing about the atonement underneath it. The children will help you turn over the snowflakes one at a time. If a piece of the repentance process is uncovered, you will help them understand what it means. If a song is uncovered, they will sing it before moving to the next snowflake.

After all the snowflakes have been turned over, briefly review steps of repentance and share your testimony of gratitude for the Atonement that can always help you be clean and pure as new snow.

Sing:
He Sent
His Son
34

Sing:
Keep the
Commandments
146

Sing:
Help Me
Dear Father
99

Sing:
Repentance
98

Keep the
Commandments

Sing:
To Think
About Jesus
71

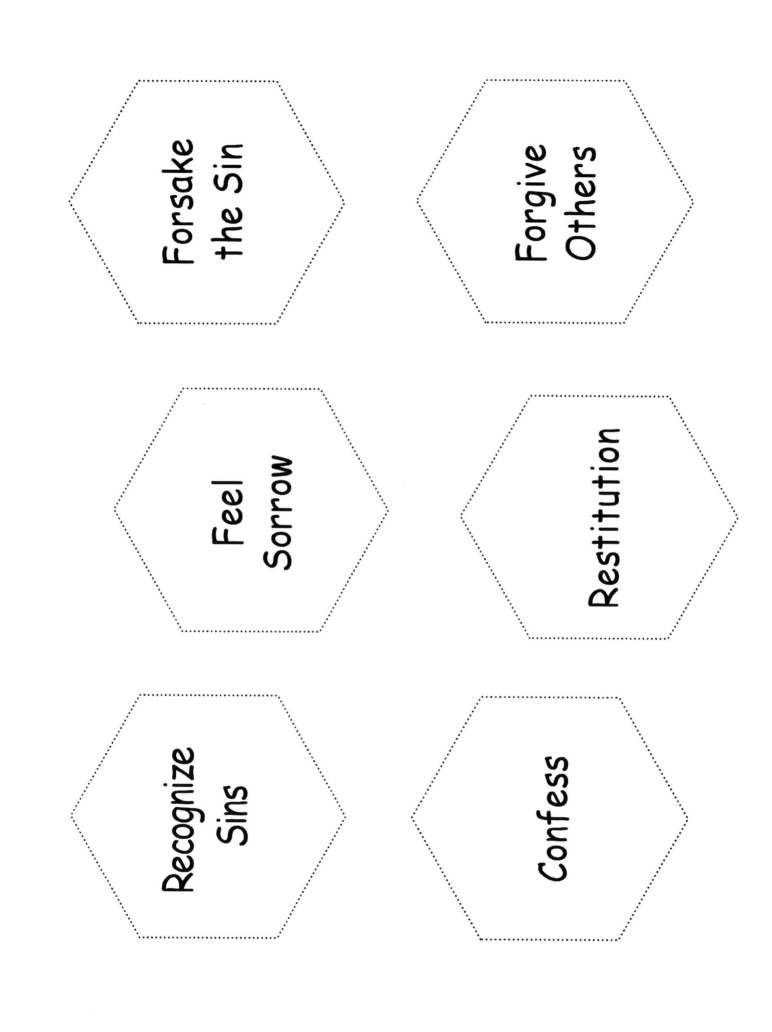

Forsake
the Sin

Forgive
Others

Feel
Sorrow

Restitution

Recognize
Sins

Confess

9. Baptism

Children's Songbook, 100

Opening Song: "This Is My Beloved Son," *Children's Songbook,* 76
Closing Song: "Baptism," *Children's Songbook,* 100

Materials Needed

- Gospel Art Kit (GAK) 208 (John the Baptist Baptizing Jesus)
- Copies of the word stanzas, enough for each class to have a set
- 24 envelopes
- Scissors
- Tape
- Marking pen
- Scriptures for the children to use
- Chalk and chalkboard

Preparation

- Be familiar with the following scriptures: Matthew 3:13–17, Mark 1:9–11, and 2 Nephi 31:5, 12.
- Separate the word strips by verse.
- Cut the strips apart and place each set in an envelope.
- Mark each envelope according to the verse it contains.

Teaching Suggestions

Begin by showing the children your GAK picture and ask them to tell you about it. Explain that you will read the story from the scriptures with them, and then they must tell it back to you in order. Have them repeat the important events from the scriptures back to you. Commend them for their efforts.

Next, explain that what they have learned will help them also learn a new song. Separate the children into their classes and give each group an envelope. Have them work together, with their teacher's help as needed, to place the words to the song in the correct order to tell the story of Jesus' baptism. Have your pianist quietly play the song in the background while they work.

When they have completed their task, review the words with them, making sure everyone has them in the right order. Tell them that these words to the story are also the first verse of the song. Repeat the words together as a whole, then let the children listen to the melody again. Point out the running notes that make the song almost feel like gently flowing water. They can sway their bodies and pretend that they are at the river Jordan when Jesus came to be baptized. Have them try to sing the first verse several times.

Next, give each class envelopes for the second verse and tell them to see if they can finish the story while the pianist again plays quietly for them. When the children think they have completed the puzzle, go over the word order and discuss the differences between the ways the story is worded in the scriptures and how the song explains the same message.

Repeat the words together several times, then let the children sway and try to sing the second verse.

Spend a few moments talking about why Jesus asked to be baptized. He needed to do everything that Heavenly Father has asked each of us to do so that He could be our example. Baptism is an important step in being able to return to Heavenly Father for all of us, even Jesus Christ. With that in mind, ask the children what they think the third verse to the song might talk about.

Explain that the last verse tells us that we need to follow the example we have been given. Read 2 Nephi 31:5, 12 with the children, then challenge them to see if they can arrange the words to the last verse of the song. Hand out the envelopes and let them work with the background music for a few minutes.

When they have finished reviewing the words as before, let the children practice the phrasing. This time as they sing, they will sway and pretend that they are in the baptismal font preparing for their own baptism. Ask the older children to try to remember what feelings they had on their baptism day. Younger children may think about what they would like that time to be like. Have them sing and sway with the last verse as well.

Briefly review all that they have discussed about baptism and the words to all three verses of the song. Show them the picture of Jesus one more time, and then ask them to closer their eyes, fold their arms, and gently sway as they think about Jesus and try to sing the song from beginning to end.

Commend them for their hard work in learning the messages of the new song. Be mindful of the spirit in the room while you encourage the children to remember how good it feels to think about Jesus and do what He commands by being baptized and by trying to live a clean life so that we all can return to live with Heavenly Father and Jesus Christ again.

word strips

Verse 1

Jesus came to John the Baptist,

In Judea long ago,

And was baptized by immersion

In the River Jordan's flow.

Verse 2

"To fulfill the law," said Jesus,

When the Baptist questioned why,

"And to enter with my Father

In the Kingdom up on high."

Verse 3

Now we know that we must also

Witness faith in Jesus' word,

Be baptized to show obedience,

As was Jesus Christ, our Lord.

("Baptism," *Children's Songbook*, 100)

10. The Desires of our hearts

Opening Song: "If You're Happy," *Children's Songbook,* 266
Closing Song: "When I Am Baptized," *Children's Songbook,* 103

materials needed

- Gospel Art Kit (GAK) 309 (Alma Baptizes in the Waters of Mormon)
- Multiple copies of the Book of Mormon for the children to use
- Copies of the heart illustrations, front and back
- Copy of the situation song references
- Chalkboard or other display area
- Tape
- Marker or pen

preparation

- Prayerfully read Mosiah 18:1–17.
- Cut out the hearts.
- Laminate the hearts for durability as desired.
- Post the hearts, blank-side up, on the chalkboard.

Teaching suggestions

Begin by showing the children the picture of Alma at the Waters of Mormon. Ask them to tell you what the picture shows.

Next, ask the children to follow along with you as you read Mosiah 18:1–17 to them. Prompt them to listen carefully because they will need to identify some of the things they heard.

After you have read the verses, ask the children if they can recall some of the things Alma told the people that were reasons for wanting to be baptized. Allow them to share their answers.

Ask them if they can recall what the people's response was to Alma's invitation to be baptized. (They clapped for joy and said this was the desire of their hearts.)

Explain that you will continue to review the blessings of baptism. Reverent children will be called forward to turn over the hearts on the chalkboard. When a heart is turned over, read the situation off of the back to the children. If the heart says something good associated with baptism, the children should clap for joy and then sing the corresponding song listed in the lesson. Briefly discuss any concepts that appear difficult for the children to understand. Verses from Mosiah 18:1–17 that can be used to reinforce the concept are located behind the positive situations.

If the heart states an unrighteous desire, the children should raise their hands with their thumbs pointed downward.

Leave each heart turned around after it is chosen.

End with your testimony of baptism and the covenants we make with Heavenly Father.

proposed situation and song coordination

- You want to be a member of The Church of Jesus Christ of Latter-day Saints (v. 8). Sing: "Little Lambs So White and Fair," *Children's Songbook*, 58.
- You want to take the name of Christ and be called one of His people (v. 8). Sing: "The Church of Jesus Christ," *Children's Songbook*, 77.
- You are willing to bear other's burdens and help them (v. 8). Sing: "A Special Gift Is Kindness," *Children's Songbook*, 145.
- You want to mourn with those who are sad (v. 9). Sing: "I'll Walk with You," *Children's Songbook*, 140.
- You want to provide comfort to others (v. 9). Sing: "I'm Trying to Be like Jesus," *Children's Songbook*, 78.
- You want to stand as a witness of God at all times, and in all things, and in all places (v. 9). Sing: "Stand for the Right," *Children's Songbook*, 159.
- You want to live with Heavenly Father and have eternal life after you die (v. 9). Sing: "Did Jesus Really Live Again?" *Children's Songbook*, 64.
- You want to serve Heavenly Father and keep His commandments (v. 10). Sing: "Keep the Commandments," *Children's Songbook*, 146.
- You want to have the Holy Ghost (v. 10). Sing: "The Holy Ghost," *Children's Songbook*, 105.
- You think being baptized will make you more popular.
- You like coming to the Primary activities.
- The missionaries are cute.
- Your best friend is a member of the Church.
- You think being baptized looks like fun.

You want to be a
member of The Church of
Jesus Christ of
Latter-day
Saints
(v.8)

You want to take the
name of Christ and be
called one of
His people
(v.8)

You are willing to
bear other's burdens
and help them
(v.8)

You want
to mourn with
those who
are sad
(v.9)

You want to
provide comfort
to others
(v.9)

You want to stand as a
witness of God at all
times and in all
things and in
all places
(v.9)

You want to live
with Heavenly Father
and have eternal
life after you die.
(v.9)

You want to serve
Heavenly Father
and keep His
commandments
(v.10)

You want
to have the
Holy Ghost
(v.10)

You think being
baptized looks
like fun

You think it will
make you more
popular

You like coming
to Primary
activities

The missionaries
are cute

Your best friend
is a member of
the Church

11. Seek the Lord early

Children's Songbook, 108

Opening Song: "Teach Me to Walk in the Light," *Children's Songbook,* 177
Closing Song: "Seek the Lord Early," *Children's Songbook,* 108

materials needed

- 2 copies of the included word search puzzle if you hold separate sharing times
- 1 copy of the included word strips
- Highlighter
- Tape or other appropriate fasteners
- Chalk and chalkboard

preparation

- Cut apart the word strips, keeping them in the order used in the song.
- Post the word search on the chalkboard or other visible area.

Teaching suggestions

Introduce this song through its title. Ask the children what they think the song will be about and have them share their own ideas about how each of us can learn to seek the Lord. Explain that you will be discussing some of these ideas as you learn the song. Show the children the prepared word puzzle. Explain that important words from the song are hidden in the puzzle, and as they find each word you will talk a little bit about it and learn a new portion of the song. When the puzzle is complete, they will have lots of ideas about how they can seek the Lord every day, as well as having learned the new song.

Post the first word strip and ask the children how they think it would fit in the song. Explain that the phrase "I'll seek the Lord early" is the first statement in the song, but it is used many times to remind the children that these are all things they can do right now. They do not need to wait until they are older to learn about Heavenly Father and gain a testimony of His gospel. Identify which word is hidden in the story for the children. (It is in bold letters as shown in the lesson reference.) Invite a reverent child to come up and search through the puzzle for the hidden key word while other children sing this first phrase to the song, and then hum along with the rest of the music. The challenge is to see if the child can find the key word in the puzzle and mark it with the highlighter before the other children reach the end of the song. Junior Primary members will choose an adult partner to help them locate the word efficiently. If a word hasn't been found by the time the known part is finished, the children must continue to hum through the rest of the song, repeating again from the beginning if necessary.

Repeat this process with each word on the list, adding to the known phrases to be sung while the word is searched for, continuing through to the end by following the melody by some other means such as humming, "oohing," or using "la." Remember to spend a moment or two discussing each new phrase's meanings with the children as it is appropriate. You may also add other ways to sing the song as the process goes along, such as having only boys or girls sing, singing while standing, or clapping, or any other interesting activity if the children get bored with the repetitive process.

After the last word on the list is found, tell the children that there is one more secret word in the puzzle. Without telling them what it is, challenge a teacher or leader to come up and see if he can find the secret word (*testimony*) before the children finish singing the entire song. If the song still needs work in some area or if the children aren't singing well, the teacher can pretend that he is unable to find the word. The children must sing again, offering their best effort to cheer him on in finding the secret word.

Explain to the children that the word *testimony* represents the message of the entire song. Using the activities listed in the song allows us to seek and find the Lord. Seeking and finding the Lord helps us become closer to Heavenly Father. It also builds our testimony and our relationships with Heavenly Father and Jesus Christ. These are the greatest things that any of us can seek for in this life.

End with your testimony of encouragement for the children's ability to seek the Lord in their own lives using the messages they've talked about today in the song.

WORD FIND

EARLY
HELP
YOUTH
TRUTH
EARLY
SCRIPTURES
FATHER
PRAYER
EARLY
OBEY
PROPHETS
COMMANDMENTS
LOVE
FOUND
TESTIMONY

word clues and corresponding phrases

"I'll seek the Lord **early**"

"While in my **youth**,"

"And he will **help** me"

"To know the **truth**."

"I'll search the **scriptures**"

"And find him **there**,"

"Then go to our **Father**"

"In fervent **prayer**."

"I'll seek the Lord **early**,"

"And I'll **obey**"

"His living **prophets** in all they say"

"I'll keep his **commandments**;"

"His **love** will abound."

"I will seek the Lord **early**,"

"And he will be **found**."

("Seek the Lord Early," *Children's Songbook*, 108)

```
W  T  S  P  R  A  L  S  X
G  F  O  R  H  O  D  C  T
K  A  O  O  B  E  Y  R  E
J  T  E  P  R  S  L  I  Y
T  H  R  H  U  C  E  P  F
H  E  C  E  F  O  A  T  H
T  R  U  T  H  M  R  U  K
R  E  A  S  N  M  L  R  L
L  G  S  P  R  A  Y  E  R
Y  O  U  T  H  N  W  S  S
F  K  C  H  I  D  J  H  E
W  U  N  F  G  M  K  F  A
E  A  R  L  Y  E  O  C  R
H  B  F  O  U  N  D  N  L
G  K  N  V  M  T  W  K  Y
Z  C  J  E  F  S  H  G  Q
```

truth

help

youth

early

scriptures

there

Father

prayer

commandments

prophets

obey

early

testimony

found

early

love

12. growing my family garden

Opening Song: "Little Purple Pansies," *Children's Songbook, 244*
Closing Song: "Seek the Lord Early," *Children's Songbook, 108*

materials needed

- Copies of the scriptures for the children to use
- Chalk and chalkboard
- Large flower vase
- A variety of silk or real flowers, 20 in all
- Masking tape
- Copy of activities for the principles, listed below
- Marker or pen

preparation

- Place a small piece of masking tape on each flower and label it with a number, one through twenty.
- Flowers can be laid on a table or piano top, or held upright in a block of foam.

teaching suggestions

Review with the children what they have learned so far about families and their importance. Tell them that today you will talk about four things that are very important for each person to remember as they try to help their family be eternal.

Write *Faith*, *Prayer*, *Repentance*, and *Forgiveness* across the top of the chalkboard. Ask the children to voice their thoughts on whether these things apply to families. Tell them that these four principles can help our families become closer and gain a more eternal perspective.

Learning and growing as families is like carefully tending a garden. If we take care of it, give it plenty of sunlight, water, and nourishment, and remove the things that don't belong, we will be rewarded with a beautiful garden. We can do the same things for our families and we will be rewarded with greater happiness and love for each other that can last forever.

Show the children the empty vase and flowers. Tell them that they will help you choose flowers to place in the vase to make a beautiful arrangement. Invite children to take turns picking flowers at random for you to put in your vase. As each flower is chosen, have the children complete the corresponding activity. They will be singing songs, searching for scriptures, and discussing different family situations to determine which gospel principle applies to each one. As each activity is completed, write it under the appropriate column on the chalkboard.

End with your testimony of these important gospel principles. Remind the children that utilizing these things can make us strong individually and as a family. Each time we nurture these gifts from Heavenly Father, we create something beautiful that can last for eternity.

FAITH

1. "Faith," *Children's Songbook*, 96
2. "God's Love," *Children's Songbook*, 97
3. "Nephi's Courage," *Children's Songbook*, 120
4. "I Know My Father Lives," *Children's Songbook*, 5
5. Hebrews 11:1
6. A father has lost his job, and he is unsure if he will be able to get another one.

PRAYER

7. "I Pray in Faith," *Children's Songbook*, 14
8. "Love Is Spoken Here," *Children's Songbook*, 190
9. James 1:5–6
10. Psalm 55:17
11. A teenage son seems to be experiencing some problems that his parents aren't sure they can help with.

REPENTANCE

12. "Repentance," *Children's Songbook*, 98
13. "The Fourth Article of Faith," *Children's Songbook*, 124
14. "Help Me, Dear Father," *Children's Songbook*, 99, verse 2
15. Psalm 38:18
16. Two sisters have been fighting all day, and it's been really awful. How can they make it better?

FORGIVENESS

17. "Help Me, Dear Father," *Children's Songbook*, 99, verse 1
18. Matthew 6:14–15
19. Ephesians 4:32
20. Your little brother gave your bike a flat tire when you let him ride it. He didn't mean to, but you don't ever want him to play with your things again.

13. my eternal Family

Annette Dickman, "My Eternal Family," *2009 Outline for Sharing Time and the Children's Sacrament Meeting Presentation* (Salt Lake City: The Church of Jesus Christ of Latter-day Saints, 2008), 10–11.

Opening Song: "Home," *Children's Songbook,* 192
Closing Song: "My Eternal Family," *CSMP Outline 2009,* 10–11

materials needed

- Copies of the included illustrations on cardstock
- Scissors
- Masking Tape
- Display table
- Hammer
- Screwdriver
- Tape measure
- Pliers
- Wrench
- Level
- Package of nails
- Package of screws
- Chalk and chalkboard
- Doctrine and Covenants

preparation

- Place a small piece of tape on one side of each tool and number them one through ten.
- Place the tools number-side down on the display table.
- Write the word to the song on the chalkboard and divide as suggested in the lesson. Do not include the chorus.

Teaching suggestions

Introduce this lesson by drawing the children's attention to your display of tools. Ask them to tell you what they are and what types of things they can be used for. Briefly discuss their ideas. Next, read D&C 88:119. Tell the children to listen carefully in order to tell you something that Heavenly Father wants each of us to build. Heavenly Father wants us each to build homes where His spirit can be present. The scripture talks about the kinds of things we can build into our own homes in order to help create eternal families. Ask them to see how many things they can recall the scripture mentioning.

Tell the children that the song they will be learning talks about building eternal families. It will also give some ideas and thoughts about how we can try to strengthen the bonds in our families and help each other get back to Heavenly Father as a family unit.

Recite the chorus for the children. Let them say it with you, then listen to the melody from the piano. Sing the chorus several times until the children are comfortable with the words and melody.

Then, explain that the chorus has a different rhythm and sound to it than the verses to the song. The chorus tells us that we can all build eternal families, but the verses will talk about the actual building process. The verses are where the children will learn what kind of tools they will need to build a family instead of just a house. Let the children hear the melody for the verses. Then, help the children find the new rhythm by using their hands to "hammer" out the beat of the song as they would in "The Wise Man and the Foolish Man" (beats 1 and 3).

Next, direct the children's attention to the words of the song that you wrote on the chalkboard. Go through each phrase on the board, discussing what it means and placing the corresponding house piece behind the phrase. Repeat the words with the children and have them try to sing as they continue to hammer out the rhythm. Continue through rest of song in this manner, singing from the beginning and adding each new portion of the house as the corresponding phrase has been discussed and practiced. At the end of each verse, combine all the phrases, along with the chorus, and have the children try singing the verse from beginning to end. Remind them to keep their hammers still while they sing the chorus.

Tell the children that you are going to test their knowledge of the new song and what they have learned about building families by identifying phrases to be erased from the board. Explain that for each phrase that can be mastered and sung in place without the words on the board earns that piece of the house. When all the pieces have been earned, the children will have all the tools and pieces they will need to construct your house puzzle. Number the front of the phrases that correspond with pieces of the house one through ten.

Call on a reverent child to tell you one thing they have learned to do in order to build an eternal family. They can then come up to choose a tool from the display table. Turn the tool over and read off the number there. Then match the number to the phrase that is to be removed, review the words, erase them, and see if the children can sing the entire song without the words there. If the children sing well, that piece of the house is placed in the "building lot" on the other side of the chalkboard.

Remove the used tool from the display table and continue until all the tools have been removed and all the pieces have been earned.

Assemble the house while reviewing what each piece stood for. Remind the children that they are important builders every day in the things they do for their families. Encourage them to choose their tools and building materials wisely.

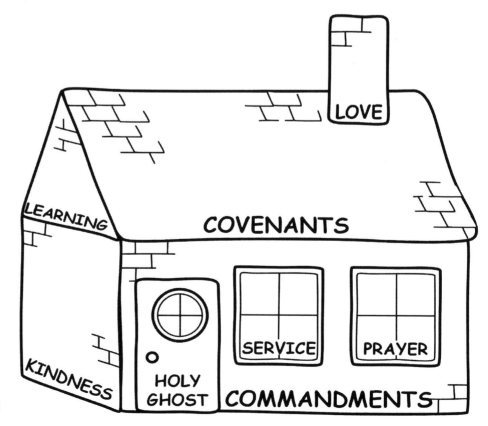

suggested song Phrases

"I am a builder working each day to build my family."

1. "And I will do the best I can to serve them lovingly." (House piece: love)

2. "I am a builder growing so tall and learning ev'ry day" (House piece: learning)

3. "To speak with kindness in my home," (House piece: kindness)

4. "To help at work and play." (House piece: service)

Chorus

"I am a builder building a home,"

5. "I seek the Lord in prayer." (House piece: prayer)

6. "And as I try to live God's word I feel the Spirit there." (House piece: Holy Ghost)

7. "I am a builder serving the Lord and following His plan" (House piece: commandments)

8. "To help my fam'ly come back home and live with Him again." (House piece: covenants)

Chorus

("My Eternal Family," *CSMP Outline 2009,* 10–11)

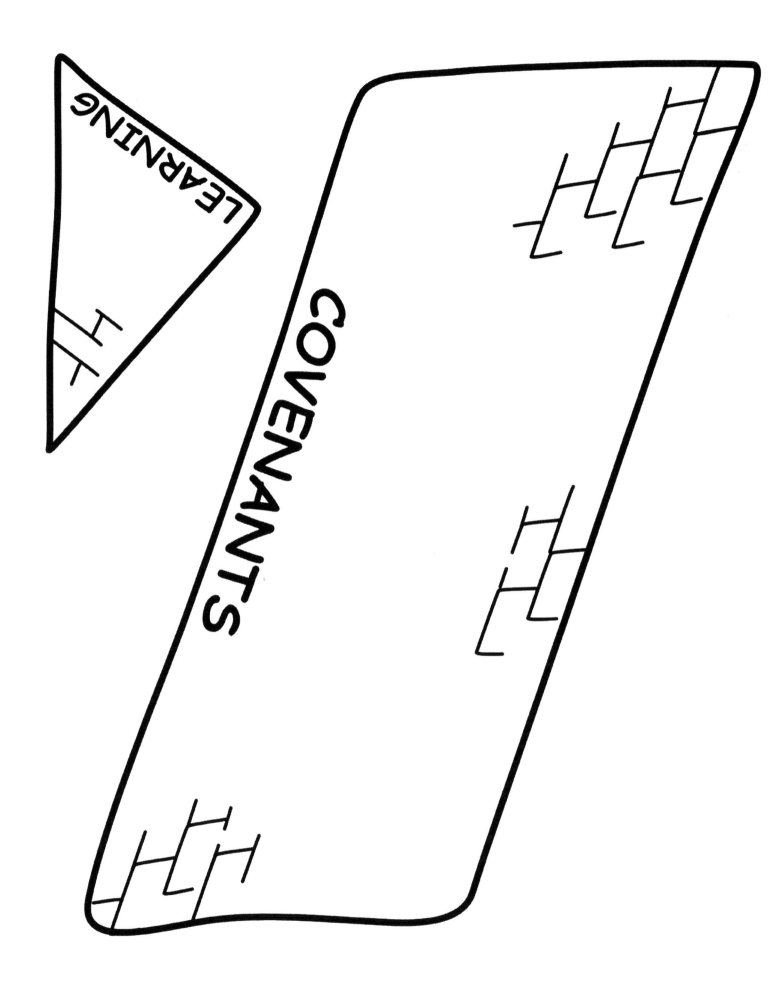

SERVICE

PRAYER

COMMANDMENTS

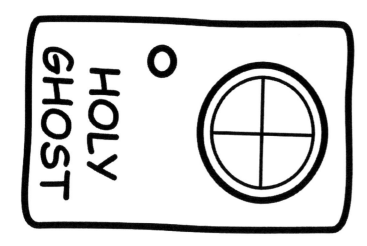

HOLY GHOST

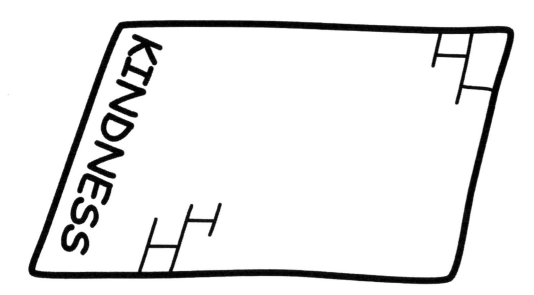

KINDNESS

LOVE

14. The Reverent Bees

Opening Song: "Father, I Will Reverent Be," *Children's Songbook, 29*
Closing Song: "Reverence Is Love," *Children's Songbook, 31*

materials needed

- 1 copy of the bee pictures on cardstock
- Copies of the "bee" reverent handout for each child
- 4 large craft sticks
- Glue
- Chalkboard and chalk
- 2 copies of the bee family story
- 12-inch chenille craft wires (stems)—1 yellow, 1½ black, and ½ white wires for each child
- Pencils for the children to use
- Craft scissors suitable for cutting chenille craft wires
- Bible

preparation

- Color, cut, and laminate the illustrations.
- Glue each bee illustration to the end of a craft stick.
- Be familiar with the story provided in this lesson.
- Give a copy of the story to the pianist so they know which songs to play at each interval.
- Practice making a chenille bee, so that you can give clear instructions.

teaching suggestions

Introduce this lesson by reading Leviticus 19:30 to the children. Ask the children to tell you what they think this scripture means. Allow them to share their answers and commend them for their thoughts.

Have the children make a list of reverent behaviors they should use in church, including the items they sang about in the opening song. Write their ideas on the chalkboard.

Tell the children that you will share a story with them about the Bee family. As they listen, the story will help remind them about the importance of being reverent while they are in Heavenly Father's house.

Share the story of the Bee family with the children. Show the picture of each bee when you reach their portion of the story and use the pauses, as directed in the story, to introduce each song that encourages reverence. The pianist will first play the beginning lines of the song. As the children recognize it, they are encouraged to hum along. Stop when most of the children are humming and ask them to reverently identify the song they have been humming. Sing the song when cued to in the next few lines of the story.

Close with your testimony of the ability of the Spirit to touch our hearts when we show proper reverence and respect for our meeting houses.

Help the children make chenille craft wire reverent bees and give each child an "I Can Bee Reverent" tag to encourage them to try to be more reverent while in the church.

The Story of the Bee Family

When the Bee family flew into the church hive on Sunday, they were all a little excited. This was going to be a special day!

The Bee family was doing an experiment.

Father Bee had given a lesson in family home evening about what a blessing it was to go to church each Sunday. He explained that when the family goes to church, they are being invited into Heavenly Father's house. Heavenly Father is almost always home, but not everyone will know He's there. Sometimes what a bee brings with them, or how they act while they are in the church hive, determines whether or not they will feel His presence.

Father Bee challenged each of his children to try and find one way that they could improve their actions at church. He promised them that if they could become reverent bees, they would feel how special it was to come to church.

The Bee family had four children: Runner, Eyespy, Gabby, and Jester. As you can imagine, their names fit them perfectly.

Runner liked to run and jump and skip everywhere he went. Now, this may seem unusual for a bee, but Runner liked the way it made his legs tickle. Running isn't bad, but sometimes Runner forgot to slow down when he was in the church hive.

Eyespy liked to see everything that was going on. She didn't want to miss a thing that was happening around her. Seeing isn't bad. In fact, Eyespy usually saw lots of things before the other bees did. Eyespy could find the flowers with the sweetest nectar, and she noticed when it was going to rain long before the other bees. But sometimes Eyespy was so busy looking around that she forgot to do other things she was supposed to do—like close her eyes and bow her head when the prayers were given in church.

Gabby just liked to gab. She talked about everything. She talked nonstop! She told stories, sang songs, and asked questions to just about anybody who would listen. The problem was Gabby had trouble stopping talking, even when other people might be saying something important.

Jester was the clown of the Bee family. He loved to make people laugh. He had a million jokes to tell and could usually find something fun in any situation. This made the people around Jester happy. Jester also knew that there were times he shouldn't laugh and joke. Sometimes he could stop himself from saying something out loud, but once a thought entered his head, a giggle or two was sure to escape!

All the Bee children knew that they were supposed to be reverent at church. It was just that sometimes it was really hard.

Not today! Today was special. Mother Bee had promised them that if they could try their very best to be reverent and respect Heavenly Father's house, they would make honey cookies after church. Father Bee promised them that the happy feelings they would get from being reverent would be even better than honey cookies.

To help them reach their goal, Mother Bee sang the children some songs about reverence.

Bees love to hum and Mother thought that if they could hum these songs they would remember the words. If they remembered, the words to the songs would help her children remember how they should act while they were in Heavenly Father's house.

Almost immediately after entering the hive, Runner saw some of his friends and almost ran to catch up with them. Fortunately he was still humming one of Mother's songs. (Have the pianist begin playing "Two Happy Feet," *Children's Songbook*, 270, for the children to hum.)

While he hummed Runner remembered these words. (Sing: "Two Happy Feet," *Children's Songbook*, 270.)

This stopped Runner in his tracks. He knew he would see his friends soon and that he should always walk when he was in the church hive. It made him happy that he remembered what he needed to do. That happiness stayed with him all day and helped him remember everywhere he went that day to hum his song. (Ask the children to tell you what Runner learned from his song.)

Eyespy didn't really have a problem until it was time for the sacrament. She loved to watch the priest bees as they broke the bread and smoothed the white tablecloths; she especially loved to see what they were doing when they knelt down to say the prayers. But, just as the prayer was about to begin, she caught herself humming. (Have the pianist begin playing "When I Go to Church," *Children's Songbook*, 157, for the children to hum.)

Just in time Eyespy remembered what the song said she should do when it was time for the prayer. (Sing: "When I Go to Church," *Children's Songbook*, 157, verse 2.)

Eyespy bowed her head and closed her eyes. When the prayer was over, Eyespy felt a wonderful peace. Suddenly she realized that it didn't matter what anyone else was doing during the prayer, she liked that feeling of peace that told her Heavenly Father was listening. (Ask the children to tell you what Eyespy learned from her song.)

Gabby was having a very difficult time. Her best friend was sitting beside her in Primary. She hadn't seen her all week and there was so much to talk about. She was trying her best, but even when she remembered to be quiet, her friend wanted to talk. When this happened, Gabby would just smile and start quietly humming again. (Have the pianist begin playing "The Chapel Doors," *Children's Songbook*, 156, for the children to hum.)

On the way to their class Gabby taught her friend the words so they could help each other listen respectfully. (Sing: "The Chapel Doors," *Children's Songbook*, 156.)

Their teacher gave a wonderful lesson about Jesus visiting the Americas. Gabby could just feel how happy the people must have been to see the Savior. It reminded her how much she loved Jesus, and the happy feeling stayed with her the rest of the day. (Ask the children to tell you what Gabby learned from her song.)

Jester came to church very happy, and it was a little hard for him to concentrate on what was going on. The first speaker had told a joke, and Jester wanted to remember it for later. The problem was every time he thought about it, a little giggle would try to escape. Jester tried to hum instead. (Have the pianist begin playing "The Things I Do," *Children's Songbook*, 170, verse 3, for the children to hum.)

It got even harder in Primary when the teacher asked if anyone had any questions. Jester didn't have a question, but the joke he kept thinking about reminded him of a story he'd like to tell the rest of his class. Instead of raising his hand to tell the story, Jester pictured the Savior in his mind teaching the people. He knew that if Jesus were teaching him, he wouldn't want to interrupt the spirit. So Jester began to hum again. (Sing: "The Things I Do," *Children's Songbook*, 170, verse 3.)

After class the teacher thanked him for helping keep the class reverent. It felt good to know that everyone had gotten a chance to feel Heavenly Father's presence because of his behavior. (Ask the children to tell you what Jester learned from his song.)

When church was finally over, the Bee children were all excited to report their progress to their mother and father. They almost ran all the way out of the church hive, but instead they began to hum together. (Have the pianist begin playing "Father, I Will Reverent Be," *Children's Songbook*, 29, for the children to hum.)

Can you guess what words they were remembering as they hummed? (Sing: "Father, I Will Reverent Be," *Children's Songbook*, 29.)

That night there were honey cookies and milk for everyone. Plus, Father Bee had been right. The happy feelings that came from showing reverence in Heavenly Father's house stayed warm inside them long after the cookies were gone.

making a Reverent Bee

Take the long yellow and black stems and twist them together from end to end.

Fold the ends of the white chenille craft wire toward its middle, creating two small loops.

Begin wrapping the yellow and black stems tightly around a pencil, with the wraps close together. When approximately half of the stem is wrapped, place the middle of the wings underneath the next portion to be wrapped, and then continue wrapping the rest of the stem around the pencil. Apply a little extra pressure to the end of the stem to hold it in place. Gently slide your bee's body off the end of the pencil and set it aside.

Fold the remaining piece of black chenille craft wire in half. Curl each of the free ends over slightly. Slide the folded end into the open center of the bee body to create a stinger on one end and antenna on the other.

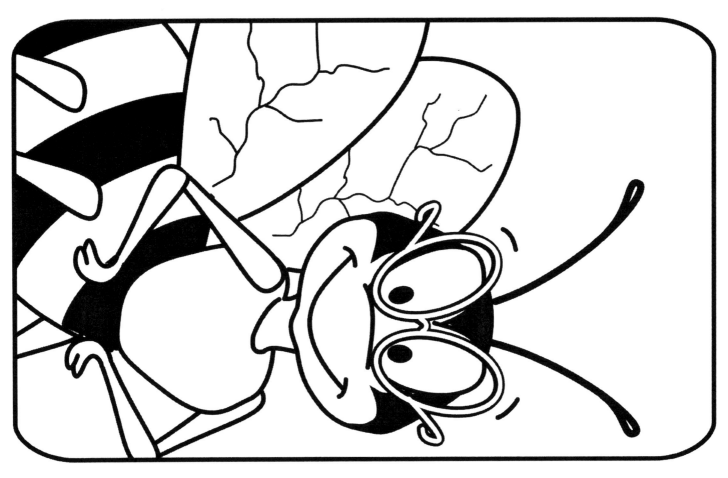

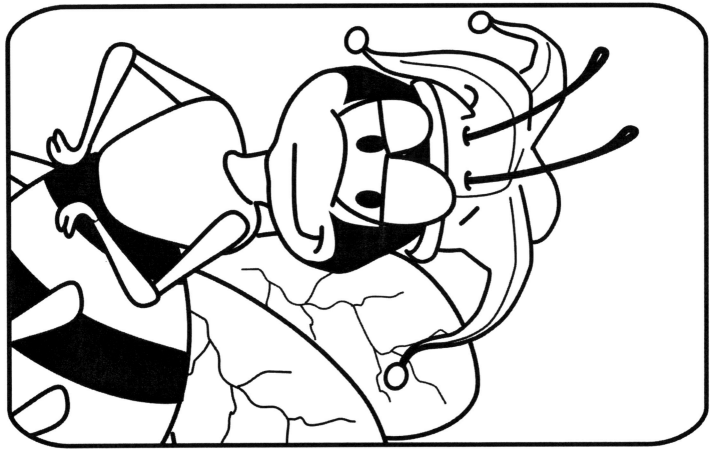

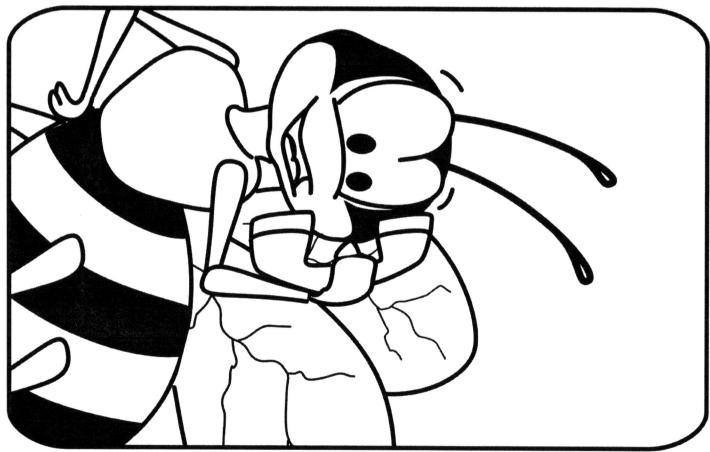

I Can

Reverent

I Can

Reverent

I Can

Reverent

I Can

Reverent

15. Families Can Be Together Forever

Children's Songbook, 188

Opening Song: "I Love to See the Temple," *Children's Songbook,* 95
Closing Song: "Families Can Be Together Forever," *Children's Songbook,* 188

Materials Needed

- Large construction paper or poster board
- A large stretchy rubber band
- Copy of illustrations for song stanzas—note that you will need 2 copies each of the family and temple illustrations
- Copy of the spinner insert
- Paper and crayons/colored pencils
- Chalkboard, chalk, and eraser

Preparation

- Color and laminate the song illustrations as desired.
- Cut the spinner insert out, also cutting on the dotted lines down to the middle of the circle and the smaller inner circle.
- Choose a spinner from a family board game (larger is better; Twister® spinners work great).
- Carefully slide the activity spinner insert underneath the board game spinner arm and lay it flat. The spinner should be able to move freely around your insert. If one cut edge sticks up and interferes, carefully tape the underside to hold it down. This allows you to remove and reuse the spinner insert.
- Cut the construction paper or poster board into an additional circle.
- Draw lines on the circle to divide it into quarters with the words *mom, dad, daughter,* and *son* written in the individual pieces.

Teaching Suggestions

Ask the children to identify the shape of your paper circle. Talk about what makes it a circle (round, no corners, never-ending). Compare the circle to an eternal family. Heavenly Father wants our families to be like circles: they should go on and on without any ends, corners, or missing pieces. All family members, such as the ones listed on your circle, are needed. You can't take one piece, or family member, out and still have a complete circle. Each person has an important part to play in their family and they must work together in the Lord's way to make the family eternal.

Each of our family circles may have more or fewer parts, but when they are all put together, every family can make an eternal circle. Discuss these comparisons and allow children to add their own ideas.

Introduce the song by showing the pictures and discussing the meaning of each line. Practice the words of the song several times with and without music.

Next, tell the children you want to show them a different kind of circle. Show the children the rubber band and ask them what makes it different from the paper circle. Let them express their answers. Then show them that the most important thing about the band is that it can grow and change. Being sealed in the temple is what makes our family a complete circle, but then we have to work and grow together if we want to be happy now and forever.

Discuss what actions make a happy family. Make a list on the chalkboard.

Discuss how some actions can make families unhappy. List these on the chalkboard also.

Show the spinner of actions and talk about how the children can show these actions. Have children hold the pictures representing the lyrics. Each child holding a picture (or an additional reverent child if your Primary is large) gets to spin for an action to do while singing that portion of the song. The chorus can be sung normally or with actions at the chorister's discretion.

Discuss that while it is fun to learn a song this way, some of these actions can really hurt the spirit of our homes. Sing the song once more using only the *peacemaker* or the *praying* action. Help the children identify the feelings of the spirit after the song is sung and encourage them to work toward feeling that spirit in their home as much as possible.

Have the children draw a circle on paper, and then draw a picture of their family inside it to remind them to strive for an eternal family.

Special note: Consider having the children draw their picture on a half sheet. Put their names on the front and collect them. Make copies of their pictures to use as the cover for your sacrament program before returning them to the children.

words and corresponding illustrations

- "I have a fam'ly here on earth. They are so good to me." (the earth)
- "I want to spend my life with them through all eternity." (circles)
- "Families can be together forever through Heavenly Father's plan." (a family)
- "I always want to be with my own family, and the Lord has shown me how I can. The Lord has shown me how I can." (temple)
- "While I am in my early years, I'll prepare most carefully," (child praying)
- "So I can marry in God's temple for eternity." (newly married couple)
- "Families can be together forever through Heavenly Father's plan." (a family)
- "I always want to be with my own family, and the Lord has shown me how I can. The Lord has shown me how I can." (temple)

("Families Can Be Together Forever," *Children's Songbook*, 188)

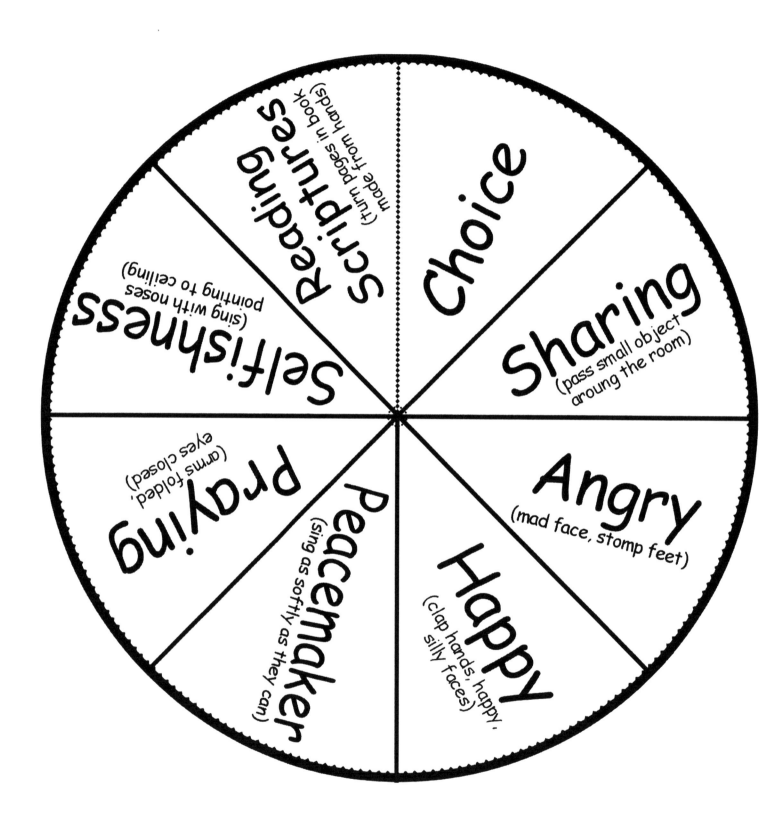

16. I have standards

Opening Song: "The Commandments," *Children's Songbook,* 112
Closing Song: "I Want to Live the Gospel," *Children's Songbook,* 148

materials needed

- Chalk and chalkboard
- 11x17 poster of "My Gospel Standards" (*Faith in God* [Salt Lake City: The Church of Jesus Christ of Latter-day Saints, 2003], back cover). (Note: GAK 618 is a slightly different version from the poster and *Faith in God* booklets. If this version is used you will not need the visual aids for Heavenly Father's plan and honoring parents)
- Copies of "My Gospel Standards" full-page size for each child
- Gospel Art Kit (GAK) 107 (Moses and the Burning Bush)
- Tape or other fasteners
- Scissors

preparation

- Mount the "My Gospel Standards" poster on one side of the chalkboard or other display area.
- Cut out the illustrated word flaps.
- Fold each word flap like a book so that the illustration is on the outside and the words are on the inside.
- Post the word flaps, with the illustration showing, randomly on the other side of the board.

Teaching suggestions

Show the children the picture of Moses. Ask them to tell you everything they can remember about this prophet. Commend them for their answers. Tell the children that Moses was given some special instructions from Heavenly Father, called commandments. These commandments were given so that Moses could tell the people exactly what Heavenly Father wanted them to do and be like.

These same commandments are still very important. Today, we not only have the Ten Commandments, but we have an additional set of guidelines to help us understand how important those commandments are. These guidelines help us understand what we can do every day to become better, happier people. They also help us prepare to make covenants with Heavenly Father, like the ones in the temple. If we are living these guidelines, we are worthy to enter Heavenly Father's house. Ask the children to guess what these other guidelines might be. Direct them toward your poster of "My Gospel Standards."

Explain that they will be learning about the things that we are all asked to do in "My Gospel Standards." You will read each phrase from the poster in order, then call up reverent children to try to find the picture that could represent the statement you read. Explain that the picture they're looking for could show a good choice about that standard or a bad one.

After the picture is located, talk about what was shown in the picture with the rest of the children. Then, open the flap to see if the statement inside matches. Discuss what choices the children can make that will help them live that standard, then sing the song noted inside the flap. Move each statement next to the poster as it has been identified so that the pictures match up with the order they appear on the poster. You can use this as a quick review method of summary at the end.

Continue this process through the entire set of standards, review the things the children have learned, and encourage them to find one standard they can practice following more carefully in the coming week as they think about being worthy to attend the temple when they are older.

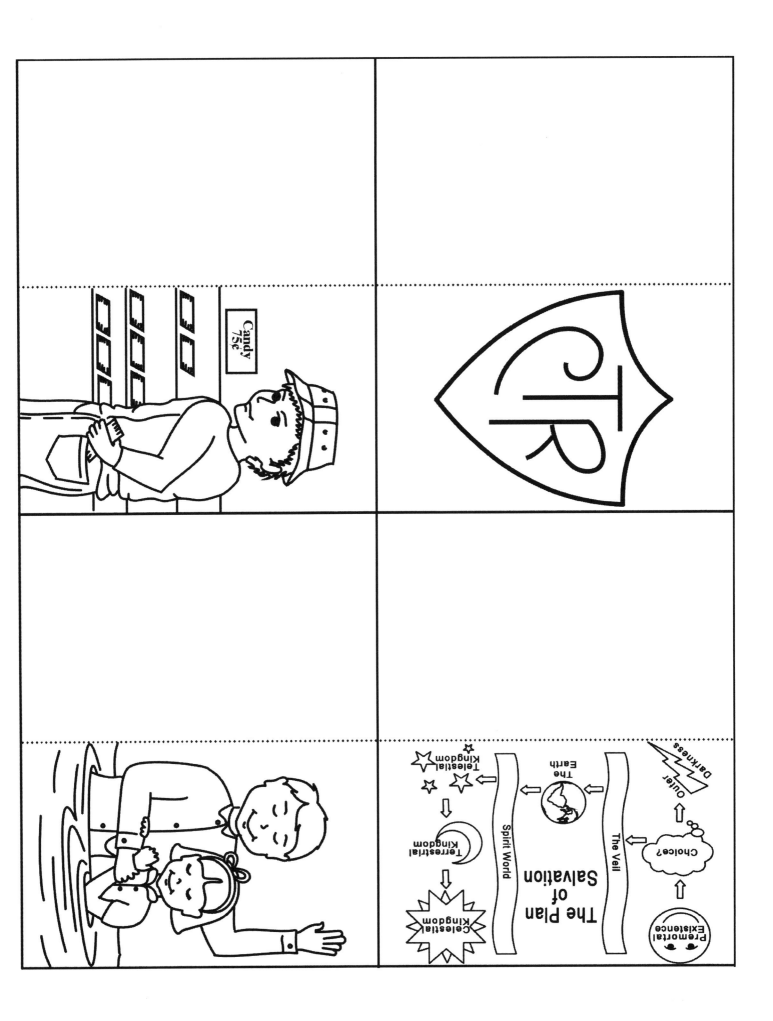

Sing:
Choose the Right Way
160

"I will choose the right. I know I can repent when I make a mistake."

Sing:
I Believe in Being Honest
149

"I will be honest with Heavenly Father, others, and myself."

Sing:
I Will Follow God's Plan
164

"I will follow Heavenly Father's plan for me."

Sing:
The Holy Ghost
105

"I will remember my baptismal covenant and listen to the Holy Ghost."

Sing:
Love Is Spoken Here
190

"I will honor my parents and do my part to strengthen my family."

Sing:
The Lord Gave Me a Temple
153

"I will keep my mind and body sacred and pure, and I will not partake of things that are harmful to me."

Sing:
Hum Your Favorite Hymn
152

"I will use the names of Heavenly Father and Jesus Christ reverently. I will not swear or use crude words."

Sing:
Remember the Sabbath Day
155

"I will do those things on the Sabbath that will help me feel close to Heavenly Father and Jesus Christ."

"I will dress modestly to show respect to Heavenly Father and myself."

Sing:
I am a Child of God
2

"I will seek good friends and treat others kindly."

Sing:
Friends Are Fun
262

"I will only read and watch things that are pleasing to Heavenly Father. I will only listen to music that is pleasing to Heavenly Father."

Sing:
The Thirteenth Article of Faith
132

"I will live now to be worthy to go to the temple, serve a mission, and do my part to have an eternal family."

Sing:
I Love to See the Temple
95

17. The Family

Children's Songbook, 194

Opening Song: "Because God Loves Me," *Children's Songbook,* 234
Closing Song: "The Family," *Children's Songbook,* 194

materials needed

- Copies of "Family Home Evening: Counsel and a Promise," *Ensign,* June 2003, 12; and "Family Home Evening," Gordon B. Hinckley, *Ensign,* Mar. 2003, 2–5
- At least 5 copies of popcorn illustrations
- Chalk and chalkboard
- Tape

preparation

- Review the information found under Gospel Topics, "family home evening," additional information section on www.lds.org.
- Be familiar with the messages from President Hinckley.
- Cut out the individual popcorn illustrations, and laminate for durability.
- Invite a guest to spend about five minutes sharing a family home evening experience that they have had with their family that helped that person feel closer to their family. This experience should be something light and uplifting.
- Write the words to the song "The Family" on the chalkboard, divided into four lines as follows:
  "When the fam'ly gets together, after evening work is done,"
  "Then we learn to know each other, popping corn and having fun."
  "Then our father tells a story, mother leads us in a song,"
  "And it seems that nothing in the world could possibly go wrong."
("The Family," *Children's Songbook,* 194)

teaching suggestions

Begin by sharing a brief bit of information about the introduction of family home evening by President Joseph F. Smith. Then, introduce your special guest and let him tell his story to the children. After your guest has shared his experience, tell the children about President Gordon B. Hinckley's experiences with family home evening when he was a child, and be sure to mention the types of things they did.

Ask the children to repeat back some of the things your guest and President Hinckley did with their families. Then, tell the children that they will be learning a song about spending time with their family. Read the words through to the children. Help them identify the similarities between the stories about family home evening that they have just heard and the words to the new song. Then, help the children repeat the words several times with you. Allow them to share their favorite parts of the words and express which of these activities happen in their own home.

Next, tell them that they need to find a clue in the song that will help them have more fun singing it. What snack does the family in the song like? (Popcorn)

Have the children describe what it sounds like when corn pops. Tell them that this song has a rhythm that is something like popping corn. Clap you hands to show the long-short-long-short pattern that repeats itself through the entire song. Let them try clapping along with you as you say the words to the song. Notice that there is longer break between each stanza but the "popping" rhythm is constant. Have the pianist play the song while the children clap along, and then add the words. Try this exercise a couple of times.

After the children are comfortable with the words and phrasing, have them take turns naming something that they like to do with their own family or naming things that can help them have better family home evenings. Each child who is singing well and gives an idea of how they enjoy being with their family can place a piece of popcorn over a word on the chalkboard. You may also randomly interject a question about the stories for the children to answer. After a handful of words have been "popped" (covered with a piece of popcorn), have the children sing the song again. Repeat this process until all the popcorn has been used or every child has had a chance to think of something they can do with their families that will bring them closer.

End with your testimony of the importance of family home evening to strengthen families. Remind the children that not every family home evening will be as memorable as the ones mentioned today, but each evening spent together add one more "kernel" of blessings that can expand to create something beautiful in our families.

Consider sending each child home with a small bag of popcorn kernels as an opener and reminder for them to talk about the things they learned regarding family home evening.

18. The Scriptures Teach About Families

Opening Song: "Families Can Be Together Forever," *Children's Songbook,* 188
Closing Song: "My Eternal Family," *CSMP Outline 2009,* 10–11

Materials Needed

- 2 copies of the included crossword puzzle on cardstock, if your unit holds separate sharing times
- 1 copy of the puzzle's solutions and corresponding information
- Marker with a thin writing tip (if your puzzle is not on cardstock use a regular pen or colored pencil)
- Tape or fasteners
- Scriptures for the children to use
- Gospel Art Kit (GAK) 103 (Noah and the Ark with Animals), 109 (Joseph Is Sold by His Brothers), 119 (Adam and Eve Teaching Their Children), 124 (Ruth Gleaning in the Fields), 204 (Flight into Egypt), 216 (Christ and the Children), 301 (Lehi's Family Leaving Jerusalem), 311 (The Anti-Nephi-Lehies Burying Their Swords), 313 (Two Thousand Young Warriors), and 321 (Conversion of Alma the Younger)

Preparation

- Post the crossword puzzle on the chalkboard or other appropriate display area.
- Be familiar with the scripture stories associated with the GAK pictures.

Teaching Suggestions

Share a brief testimony of the scriptures with the children as an introduction to the day's topic. Help the children understand that the scriptures are a guide that Heavenly Father has given us to learn from. They help us feel His spirit and understand what He wants us to do to become more like Jesus Christ. Another thing that you can learn about in the scriptures is how to strengthen our families so that they can become forever families.

Show the children your posted crossword puzzle. Explain that they will help you identify the names of people from the scriptures who can help them learn more about families. Each clue for the crossword puzzle gives a scripture that discusses things the ancient prophets have taught us about families. Read the scriptures given as the clues on the crossword puzzle with the children, one at a time. Identify the corresponding GAK picture and review the story that the scripture talked about. Emphasize the action from the scriptures that shows something that can be done to strengthen a family. Sing the corresponding song while a chosen child or leader fills in the name from the scripture that fits the puzzle.

End by encouraging the children to search their scriptures for ways that they can help and support their families.

crossword answers. coordinating gak pictures. and songs

- Alma: Mosiah 27:18–19, 22–23, GAK 321 (Conversion of Alma the Younger [prayed for his family]). Sing: "Book of Mormon Stories," *Children's Songbook*, 118, verse 3.
- Stripling Warriors: Alma 57:20–21, GAK 313 (Two Thousand Young Warriors [learned faith and obedience from mothers]). Sing: "We'll Bring the World His Truth (Army of Helaman)," *Children's Songbook*, 172.
- Anti-Nephi-Lehies: Alma 23:7, 16–17, GAK 311 (The Anti-Nephi-Lehies Burying Their Swords [repenting of sins and promising not to fight anymore]). Sing: "Repentance," *Children's Songbook*, 98.
- Joseph: Matthew 2:13–14, GAK 204 (Flight into Egypt [follow Heavenly Father's commandments and inspiration]). "The Still Small Voice," *Children's Songbook*, 106.
- Jesus: Matthew 19:13–15, GAK 216 (Christ and the Children [children are important and special]). Sing: "Jesus Loved the Little Children," *Children's Songbook*, 59.
- Lehi: 1 Nephi 2:7, 9–10, GAK 301 (Lehi's Family Leaving Jerusalem [showing gratitude and counseling children]). Sing: "Fathers," *Children's Songbook*, 209.
- Noah: Genesis 7:1, GAK 103 (Noah and the Ark with Animals [worked to provide for and protect family]). Sing: "Follow the Prophet," *Children's Songbook*, 110, verse 3.
- Joseph: Genesis 45:3–5, GAK 109 (Joseph Is Sold by His Brothers [forgives family when they hurt him]). Sing: "Help Me, Dear Father," *Children's Songbook*, 99.
- Adam: Moses 5:10–12, GAK 119 (Adam and Eve Teaching Their Children [teach children the gospel]). Sing: "Teach Me to Walk in the Light," *Children's Songbook*, 177.
- Ruth: Ruth 1:16, GAK 124 (Ruth Gleaning in the Fields [serving and helping each other]). "Go the Second Mile," *Children's Songbook*, 167.

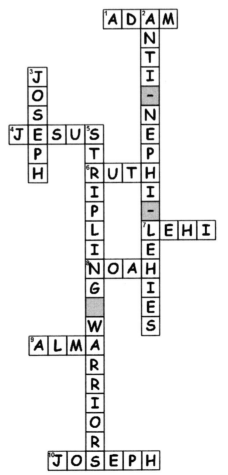

ACROSS

1. Moses 5:10-12
4. Matthew 19:13-15
6. Ruth 1:16
7. 1Nephi 2:7; 9-10
8. Genesis 7:1
9. Mosiah 27:18-19
10. Matthew 2:13-14

DOWN

2. Alma 23:7; 16-17
3. Genesis 45:3-5
5. Alma 57:20-21

19. home can Be a heaven on earth

Hymns, no. 298

Opening Song: "I Lived in Heaven," *Children's Songbook,* 4
Closing Song: "Home Can Be a Heaven on Earth," *Hymns,* no. 298

materials needed

- Heart-shaped item
- Picture of a happy child
- Small blanket
- Hammer
- *Family Home Evening Resource Book*
- Picture of a family
- Candle
- Tape measure
- Picture of a child praying
- Scriptures
- Hymnal
- Compass

preparation

- Assign children to help you teach the new song by learning a single phrase from the song (just the words, not singing it), and have them bring the corresponding item from the materials list from their own homes to use as visual aides.
- You will want to send a note home with them from church the week before, and provide a reminder phone call just before the Sunday presentation.

Teaching suggestions

Let the children stand up and present their items in random order. Each child should also share the phrase they learned to go with their item. The other children are then invited to repeat that passage of the song once.

Next, help the children find their places in the song. Start at the beginning of the song and sing the beginning phrase for the children. Without the child giving themselves away, see if the rest of the children can remember who had that phrase just by the item they're holding. When the child and item have been identified, have him come to the front of the line while the rest of the children practice singing the phrase several times. Continue rearranging the children in this manner. When the children and symbols for each verse have been assembled correctly, repeat the phrases in order. Then have the children try to sing the entire verse.

When the entire song is represented in the proper order, see if the children can remember what each item stands for and sing the entire song one more time.

Emphasize that each child has a special home with different things that make it like heaven, but each of us has a responsibility to try our best to make our homes places the Savior would like to be. That is why this song tells us many things that we can do to bring the Spirit into our homes and reminds us at the end of each verse to "make," "reach," and "lead" our homes toward heaven.

suggested words and visual aids

- "Home can be a heav'n on earth when we are filled with love," (any heart-shaped item)
- "Bringing happiness and joy, rich blessings from above—" (picture of a happy child)
- "Warmth and kindness, charity, safety and security—" (child-size blanket)
- "Making home a part of heaven, where we want to be." (hammer)
- "Drawing fam'ly near each week, we'll keep love burning bright." (FHE manual)
- "Serving Him with cheerful hearts, we'll grow in truth and light." (candle)
- "Parents teach and lead the way, children honor and obey," (picture of their family)
- "Reaching for our home in heaven, where we want to stay." (tape measure)
- "Praying daily in our home, we'll feel His love divine;" (any picture of a child praying)
- "Searching scriptures faithfully, we'll nourish heart and mind." (scriptures)
- "Singing hymns of thanks, we'll say, 'Father, help us find the way" (hymnal)
- " 'Leading to our home in heaven, where we long to stay.' " (compass)

("Home Can Be a Heaven on Earth," *Hymns*, no. 298)

20. The Family Proclamation

Opening Song: "I Love to See the Temple," *Children's Songbook,* 95
Closing Song: "Love Is Spoken Here," *Children's Songbook,* 190

Materials Needed

- Copies of "The Family: A Proclamation to the World" (*Ensign*, Nov. 1995, 102) for each class
- Dress-up clothes to represent the different members of a family talked about in the situations: father, mother, a young child, brother, sister, and teenagers.
- *Children's Songbooks* for the classes to reference
- Copy of the family situations

Preparation

- Cut apart the family situations and place them into a container or holder.
- Prayerfully read "The Family: A Proclamation to the World" and decide which portions are most important for your children to read and discuss with you.

Teaching Suggestions

Discuss how and why the First Presidency issued the proclamation. The proclamation is to help us understand what God expects of us as members of a family. Many people have forgotten how important a family is.

Have the children help you read portions of the proclamation aloud. Ask the children what they think it means. Explain any words that appear difficult for them. Then review the middle of the seventh paragraph with them again.

"Happiness in family life is most likely to be achieved when founded upon the teachings of the Lord Jesus Christ. Successful marriages and families are established and maintained on principles of faith, prayer, repentance, forgiveness, respect, love, compassion, work, and wholesome recreational activities" ("The Family: A Proclamation To The World," 102).

Divide the children into their classes, or in other appropriate groups. Have a child from each group draw a situation out of your container for his class to discuss and work out a solution to. Class members must then dress up and role-play the situation and its righteous solution for the rest of the Primary. They must also choose a Primary song that represents the persons or actions they were talking about to be sung before the next class presents their situation.

End by pulling just a few examples out of the children's role-playing efforts that showed an ability to think through and find the most righteous solution to difficult situations families can face. Encourage the children to take a moment to think about problems they are facing, just as they did today, and try to see themselves doing something to make things better for their family.

suggested family situations

- A mother and daughter disagree about when the daughter should come home from a party.
- A girl's boyfriend says he wants to marry her, but he doesn't want a temple wedding. He says that he wants her to have a big, fancy wedding where she can feel special. Besides, they can always go to the temple later.
- A family must decide whether to go to church on Sunday or begin their vacation a day early.
- Your little brother wants to play with you and your friend, but he's really a pain and never plays right.
- A pair of sisters has been fighting. Each is sure that she is right and the other is being mean and unfair.
- Your brother put a dent in dad's car, but he isn't going to tell. He says your dad will never notice or will just think he did it himself.
- Your mother is sick, but you are hungry and can't find anything you want to eat.

21. When We're Helping

Children's Songbook, 198

Opening Song: "We Welcome You," *Children's Songbook,* 256
Closing Song: "When We're Helping," *Children's Songbook,* 198

Materials Needed

- Copies of the two dice patterns
- Scissors
- Tape
- Chalk and chalkboard

Preparation

- Cut the dice out, fold them into their correct cube forms, and secure them with tape.
- Prepare a list of review questions about key family principles that have been taught in your unit over the past year.

Teaching Suggestions

Talk about service and how it can help strengthen the family. Explain that they will be learning a short song today that will help them remember how important it is to help and serve different people.

Introduce the melody and second verse first. Allow the children to sing the "la" portion along with the piano a few times until they are comfortable with the melody.

Next, remind the children that they are talking about helping people today, so the name of this song is "When We're Helping." These are also the first words to be sung. Repeat the words to the song to the following point, "When we're helping, we're happy, and we sing as we go." Practice the song to that point, one or two times.

Next ask a reverent child to name one person who is part of a family (mother, father, brother, and so on). Write their chosen family member on the chalkboard. Insert the name into the last portion of the song and teach the children the rest of the words with their chosen family member in place. Then, discuss with the children what some of their ideas would be on how they can help and serve this person. List their ideas on the chalkboard, underneath that family member's name. Then choose one or two that the children could act out with a simple movement, like sweeping the floor, or brushing hair.

Have the children practice singing the entire first verse with their chosen family member and acting out a simple act of service from their list. You might choose to have them complete a different action for a second run-through.

Repeat this process for the most common family members (father, mother, sister, brother, baby, grandma, and grandpa).

Finally, show the children the dice you prepared. Explain that you will be asking the children questions about what they have learned about eternal families over the course of the year. Reverent children who can answer the questions correctly will be called up to help you roll your dice.

Both dice will need to be rolled for each time you sing the song. The family member die will show you who to sing about in the first verse. Decide on an appropriate helping action for them to use as well. The second die will give the children different ways to sing the second verse while they continue the chosen action from the first verse.

End by reminding the children that the message of this song is that families should be happy and joyful. All the things they have been learning can help them have the eternal families Heavenly Father would like everyone to have.

The best way we can help make our homes happy is to love and care for each other. That means helping and supporting each other as much as we can, just as they showed through their actions here. Encourage the children to remember to be more mindful of ways they can help and show love for their family during the coming week.

Mother

Sister

Father

Brother

Neighbor

Choice

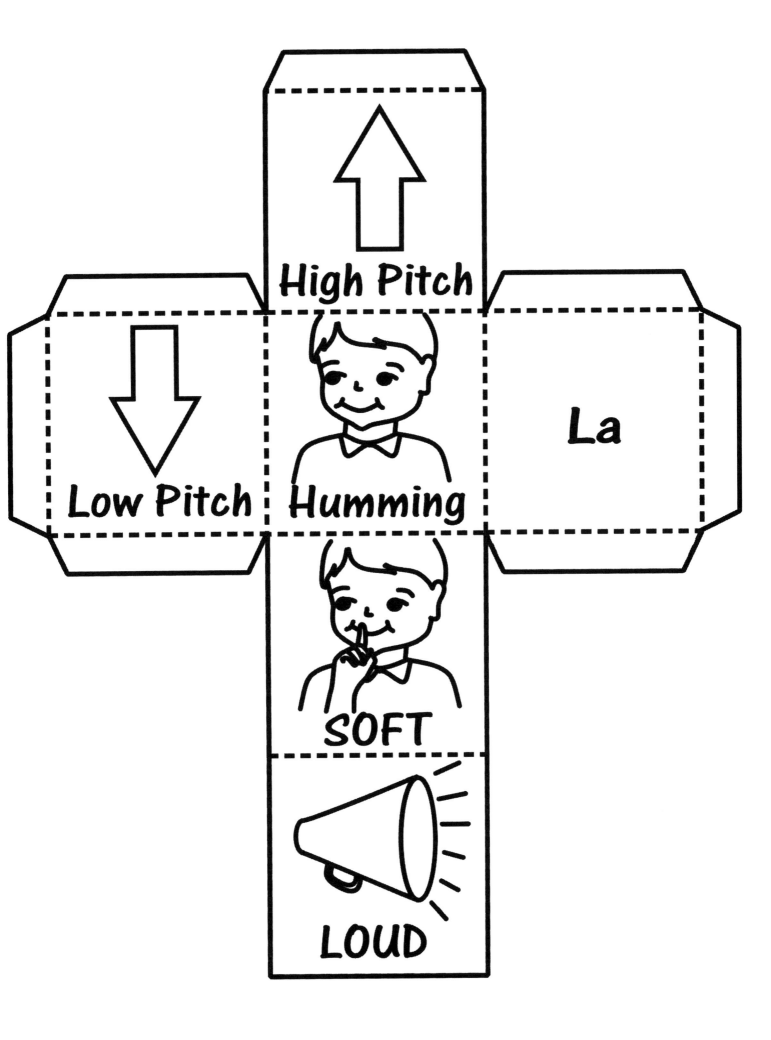

22. Mystery Moms and Dads

Opening Song: "The Dearest Names," *Children's Songbook,* 208
Closing Song: "I Am a Child of God," *Children's Songbook,* 2

Materials Needed

- Pictures of approximately 8 mothers and fathers of children in the Primary as infants or young children
- Tape or other fasteners
- 8 Ziploc® sandwich bags
- Chalkboard or other display area
- 8 index cards

Preparation

- Ask the featured parents to provide a few brief clues that might help their children identify them. They should also share a few things they learned as a child that helped them become a better parent, and include their favorite Primary song.
- Number the index cards one through eight.
- Assign each parent's information a number, one through ten.
- Place each picture inside a Ziploc® bag to protect it.
- Place the corresponding index card number behind each picture so that the number can be read from the backside of the bag.
- Mount pictures on the chalkboard facedown (numbers showing).

Note: If you hold separate junior and senior sharing times, make sure that the pictures you use are applicable to each group.

Teaching Suggestions

Tell the children that you will introduce them to some special children; each one grew up to be a parent to someone in your Primary. You will show them each picture one at a time and read the children clues about this special person. The children will try to guess whose parent it might be.

When each mother and father is guessed correctly, have the children sing that parent's favorite Primary song before going on to the next picture.

End with your testimony about the special job parents do. Each one is different, but Heavenly Father has given each of us just the right mother and father to help us grow up to be the best people we can be. Remind the children that as they choose the right and learn from their parents, they are also learning important things that will help them be good mothers and fathers when they grow up.

23. The shepherd's carol

Children's Songbook, 40

Opening Song: "Away in a Manger," *Children's Songbook,* 42
Closing Song: "The Shepherd's Carol," *Children's Songbook,* 40

materials needed

- Gospel Art Kit (GAK) 201 (The Nativity)
- Tape or digital recorder
- Medium-size nativity set
- Display table

preparation

- Arrange with the bishop, or other special ward member, to be involved in your sharing time activity. Select an appropriate spot for the children to meet with him, preferably outside of the Primary room, and arrange it appropriately.

Teaching suggestions

Show GAK 201 and ask the children what the story is. Let them help you tell the story, as each part is mentioned (Mary, Joseph, stable, manger, shepherds, and wise men). Show the corresponding piece of your nativity scene and add it to the display.

Tell the children that they will learn a song that describes the same story. Hold up each piece, this time repeating the identifying words from the song. Use the shepherd for "All God's children, come to adore" and the wise men for "Bringing gifts of love evermore."

Have the children learn and practice the music until they can sing it very well, with and without the piano.

Draw the children's attention back to your nativity scene. Remind the children that the shepherds and the wise men both had to take a journey to find Christ. Note that the wise men were not present on the night Jesus was born, but they came to find Him as soon as they were shown the way. Explain that while we may not need to leave our homes to find Christ, we each have a chance to learn and grow to become more like Christ every day. The more we try to be like Him, the more we get to know Him and feel His love for us, just as we would have felt if we could have been there when He was born.

Explain to the children that they will sing the song they just learned on a short journey. Have the children line up reverently behind you. They will quietly sing while they follow you on a special trip to meet someone who can help them grow closer to Jesus.

Sing and play "follow the leader" to the arranged point and have the children sit down around the bishop. After everyone is seated, let the bishop briefly share a picture of Jesus Christ, a special memory about Christmas as it pertains to the Savior, and his testimony with the children. When he is finished, the children must once again "follow the leader" while singing to get back to their seats.

Next, tell the children that they will need to sing the song one more time for you so that you can tape them singing it. You will then show them another way to sing "The Shepherd's Carol." Tape the children singing, then play it back for them once.

Help them understand the concept of a round and teach them what the cue is for the second group of people to start singing. In "The Shepherd's Carol," this is marked with a number two. Note that the song can be further divided into three or four parts as the children are ready for a further challenge.

Explain that you will play the tape to represent the first group and they must come in on the cue to sing as the second group. You can have the pianist lightly play along with the children's part at first, as needed. Practice this a few times, then put the tape away and divide the children into two groups for the "grand finale."

Remind them that Jesus came to earth in order to be our example and to help us return to live with Heavenly Father again. Encourage them to find ways they can bring themselves closer to Him every day.

24. Choose the Right maze

Opening Song: "Choose the Right Way," *Children's Songbook,* 160
Closing Song: "I'm Trying to Be like Jesus," *Children's Songbook,* 78

materials needed

- Copy of the blank maze on cardstock
- Copy of the maze situations for reference
- Gospel Art Kit (GAK) 240 (Jesus the Christ)
- Scissors
- Tape
- Marking pen
- Pencil
- Chalk and chalkboard

preparation

- If cardstock was not used, mount the maze on a piece of poster board or cardboard.
- Compare the blank maze to the worked maze answer key. Place a lightly penciled number (visible to you, but not to the children in their seats) at each decision point.
- Rest the large maze in the chalk tray of the chalkboard. If a chalkboard is not available, use an easel.

Teaching suggestions

Show the picture of Jesus Christ and ask the children to talk about the reasons He came to earth (to be an example, to atone for our sins, to be resurrected so we could be as well, and so forth). Remind the children that Jesus was chosen to be our Savior before we ever came to this earth. Heavenly Father knew Jesus' example and sacrifice would be the only way we would be able to return to be with Him again.

We each have an important job to do here on earth. That job is to follow Heavenly Father's plan for each of us by following the example of Jesus Christ and using the blessing of the Atonement that He gave us, in order to find our way back to Heavenly Father and the Savior in the celestial kingdom. Point out the earth and celestial kingdom on your maze. Explain that as we try to follow Jesus Christ, we are faced with many different types of choices. Remembering Jesus Christ helps us to make right choices. Even so, we won't always make the right one, but if we try to repent of the wrong choices, we can always find our way back to the path Heavenly Father wants us to follow.

Remind the children of the opening song, "Choose the Right Way." Tape your picture of the Savior above the right side of your maze as you are facing it. Then draw a small right-hand arrow with the words "choose the right" beside it. Explain that the children will be helping you work the maze by deciding if the situations you present are right choices or wrong choices. If the choice was good and something Jesus would want us to do, you will turn right on the maze. If the choice wasn't very good, you will turn left.

Draw a small arrow to the left above the left side of the maze and write "repent" beside it.

Explain that when you make a right turn, the children will sing a song that has to do with the good decision from the situation. If a left turn is made because of a wrong choice, you will stop and the children will have to suggest ways that they could exercise repentance to correct the wrong choice before moving forward in the maze again.

Begin at the picture of the earth on the bottom of the maze and draw a line with your marker until you come to your first penciled decision point. Stop and read the first situation. Get the children's answer for which direction to go, then sing or discuss the situation before continuing to mark your path through the maze until you come to the next decision point. Follow this pattern through the entire maze.

Hint: Do not fasten the maze to the chalkboard because it helps to turn and reorient the map so that each area of decision plainly diverges to the right and left you drew on the board. This helps the children to clearly see the progression and orientation. (And, so you don't get confused, either!)

End by congratulating the children for knowing how to choose the right, as well as reminding them of the power of the Atonement to help us fix any mistakes as we all try to find our way back to Heavenly Father.

maze situations and songs

1. You bring a friend to church with you. Sing: "The Things I Do," *Children's Songbook*, 170.
2. You cleaned your room without your mother reminding you. Sing: "When We're Helping," *Children's Songbook*, 198.
3. You lied about where you were going with your friends after school.
4. You fought with your sister over who got to sit in the front seat.
5. You cheated on a test at school.
6. You bought a CD that had some inappropriate music on it.
7. You paid your tithing today. Sing: "I Want to Give the Lord My Tenth," *Children's Songbook*, 150.
8. You say your prayers every night. Sing: "I Pray in Faith," *Children's Songbook*, 14.
9. You made a goal to read your scriptures every day. Sing: "Search, Ponder, and Pray," *Children's Songbook*, 109.
10. You tried the cigarette someone offered you.

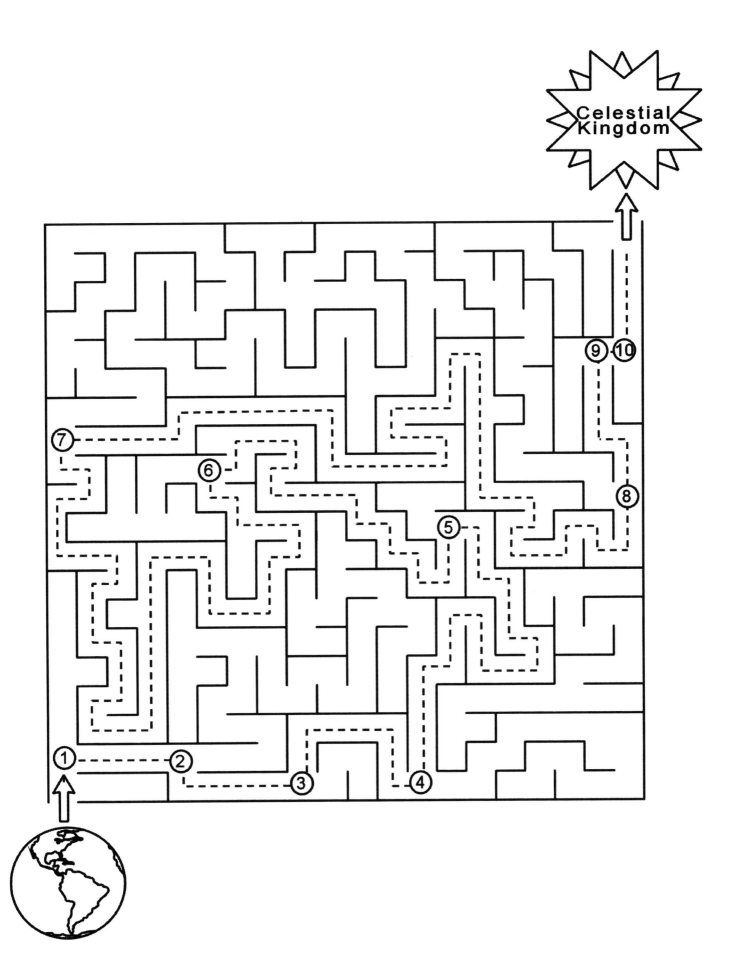

Celestial
Kingdom

Celestial
Kingdom

About the Author

ALISON PALMER is a lifelong member of the Church. Born in Mesa, Arizona, she grew up in West Virginia and graduated from Marshall University with a bachelor's degree in nursing.

Alison has held many callings in the Church, including several that have helped develop her great love for the Primary children. She has served as nursery leader, pianist, chorister, teacher, den leader, and Primary president. She has also taught Sunday School and served as a teacher and leader in Relief Society and Young Women organizations.

Writing is Alison's favorite pastime, but you can frequently find her reading, playing the piano, cooking, attending the temple, taking long walks, sewing, or playing with her family.

Alison is the author of *Sharing through Primary Songs, Volumes One, Two, Three, and Four*; *Special Occasion: Sharing Through Primary Song*; *Planting Seeds of Faith: Fun Character-building Activities for LDS Children*; and *Walking the Path of Faith: More Fun Character-building Activities for LDS Children*.

You can learn more about Alison at
WWW.AMPALMER.COM